GETTING STARTED WITH MENTORING

A PRACTICAL GUIDE TO SETTING UP AN INCLUSIVE MENTORING PROGRAM

Myrna Marofsky & Ann Johnston

PRO GROUP
PROFESSIONAL DEVELOPMENT GROUP, INC.
www.progroupinc.com

Getting Started with Mentoring:
A Practical Guide to Setting Up an Inclusive Mentoring Program
by Myrna Marofsky and Ann Johnston

Copyright © 2001
Professional Development Group, Inc., dba ProGroup®
Riverplace
One Main Street SE
Suite 200
Minneapolis MN 55414

Design by Jeanne Lee
Edited by Maren Hoven Dale

Ambassador Press
1400 Washington Avenue North
Minneapolis MN 55411

Printed on recycled paper

ISBN# 1-893030-02-4

To Sarah and Eve who taught me how to be a mentor.

M.o.M.

To my mother, Helen Johnston, who put me
in the path of my first mentor, Georgia Kitt, S.C.
I am grateful to you both.

A.J.

CONTENTS

Acknowledgements

Ann and I want to thank all of our clients and associates who provided us with valuable data to use in writing *Getting Started with Mentoring: A Practical Guide to Setting Up an Inclusive Mentoring Program.* Especially we owe gratitude to Sam Haider of Abbott Laboratories and Sandy Harris of General Mills who have trusted us and partnered with us many times to try "something different."

Over the course of our 16 years as consultants specializing in diversity, we have had the pleasure of talking to individuals at all levels of our client organizations to learn about success factors, especially for women and people of color. We conducted extensive focus groups with multicultural business associates who had been mentors or protégé/mentees themselves. This was an opportunity to concentrate on the elements of mentoring and to delve into the success factors for all individuals in today's organizations.

When we speak at conferences about our mentoring experiences, we also learn about the practices of other companies. All of this has given us the material we use to create successful programs for our clients. In addition, I have mentored, and Ann has been both a protégé/mentee and mentor while conducting research for this book. This gave us the hands-on experience needed to write about this subject.

We hope you find *Getting Started with Mentoring: A Practical Guide to Setting Up an Inclusive Mentoring Program* helpful as you begin setting up your own mentoring program.

Myrna Marofsky

How to Use This Book

This is not a cookbook for mentoring, with step-by-step recipes to assist you in setting up a mentoring program. It does, however, contain "ingredients" that can be mixed together to meet the needs of your organization. We suggest reading it all, then going back and selecting the information that will work best for your particular situation.

Every company, firm, hospital, clinic, plant or other organization has a culture all its own. The better you know the culture of your organization—its players, its politics, as well as the pathways and pitfalls for a mentoring program—the more you will see possibilities for your own situation. Because every situation is unique, comments and suggestions in this book are designed to trigger your thinking about your own organization.

Terms can vary between organizations. For example, some choose to call participants in mentoring programs "protégés" while others are called "mentees." Some call mentors "ambassadors," while others call them "sponsors." *Getting Started with Mentoring* uses "mentor" and "protégé/mentee," but feel free to adapt these terms.

We also use the term "mentoring program" to describe initiatives large and small. As we will discuss later, now that organizations are sponsoring these events, they have often been called "initiatives" to signify that they are not just here today and gone tomorrow. We have chosen "mentoring programs" to encompass the wide variety of forms mentoring can take.

As you begin establishing a mentoring program in your organization, you may become discouraged or distracted by the minutia and details involved. However, you will find that focusing on the most important aspect of the mentoring process—namely the relationship between the mentor and protégé/mentee—will help you stay on course. Stay focused on the importance of relationships and the positive impact mentoring will have on your employees and workplace as you embark on this important work.

CHAPTER ONE

Before You Begin

We are in a world where most businesses are being reinvented. It is the people in the businesses, not the people at the top of the hierarchy, who will reinvent them. It is essential to find ways to release that energy and develop leaders at all levels of the organization.

AMY WOODS BRINKLEY, BANK OF AMERICA

Since you have picked up this book, there is a high probability that you are experiencing one of three things:

1. Someone has suggested that mentoring would be good for your organization and you have been designated as the person to make it happen. You've heard a lot of noise about mentoring, but the "how to's" are missing.

2. You are in the midst of implementing or coordinating a mentoring program and want help in making it more effective.

3. You have launched a mentoring program with big fanfare, but it isn't living up to the hype or the expectations. In fact, some are questioning its viability.

The first step in a successful mentoring program—whether the concept is new, something you've tried and are marginally pleased with or a strategy that needs to be completely revamped—is to recognize its value to the organization: the business case for mentoring. The success of the program will hinge on how much and how well it addresses business issues, because that is how its success will be measured. In order to make the program successful, you will need to clarify the link between mentoring and achieving business goals around issues like productivity, innovation and addressing customer needs.

No matter how pleased participants are with the personal rewards related to the mentoring experience, the real measures of the impact of your program will be: Are participants advancing? Are they staying actively involved in the program? How do they respond on surveys? Are they reporting satisfaction?

It is getting easier to make the link between mentoring and business issues as more and more *people* are seen as a primary corporate resource. Whether your mentoring program is designed to improve your company's image, retain talented individuals or develop and motivate the "best and the brightest," you may be surprised at how much positive attention you will get when you speak about mentoring using business language. In other words, communicate that mentoring is not just a nice thing to do, but a *need* for the overall health and growth of your organization. Mentoring is about fully utilizing human potential: people's knowledge, skills, experiences and capabilities. That means having all employees, regardless of their background, culture or ethnicity working to their full potential.

The better you are at connecting business issues to mentoring and the sooner you start to do it, the more you will find champions, willing participants, resources and time—not to mention the high praise you will get for implementing a successful program.

It may also help to think of your mentoring program as if it were a "shadow factor"—always connected to the plans you make, the conversations you have and the results you measure. Throughout *Getting Started with Mentoring*, we will help you make these connections.

The ability of organizations to implement dynamic change and meet the needs of their constantly evolving markets is determined by their capacity to attract, retain and develop the skills and talents of employees. For many of these organizations, mentoring is on the top of their list when determining a strategy for addressing the imposing "war for talent." Beginning with who you select and how you match mentors and protégé/mentees, to what the structure of the program is, there must be an ability to "sell" the benefits of your mentoring program in terms of how it will impact the success of, not only the participants, but your organization as a whole.

Here's why.

Mentoring Is a Recruiting Tool

Many have learned that a key recruiting tool is the reputation the organization has and the type of workplace it provides: the opportunities it offers and the things employees say about working there. The once popular concept of being the "employer of choice" has now become being the "sought-after employer." In addition, today's employers are finding they have to "re-recruit" their current employees by stimulating their interest so they will commit to advancement and additional responsibilities.

Mentoring Is a Developmental Tool

Fortunately, there is a growing awareness of the hidden talent that lies within the ranks of organizations. Often gone untapped because individuals were not part of the exclusive "club" or because they did not meet previously held "models of success," organizations are using mentoring as a way to identify and develop talent at all levels, and in particular, are recognizing the talents of employees of color and women. Mentoring has become a way to improve employee effectiveness, help navigate careers and develop leaders, and spans the full diversity of the employee population.

Mentoring Is a Retention Tool

Organizations are reexamining their notion of who are the "best and brightest" and are implementing innovative and inclusive mentoring programs that nurture relationships critical to the success of the participants and the organization. As new and diverse employees enter the workforce, mentoring relationships help these employees navigate the waters of long-held organizational cultures so they can learn the unwritten rules for success. As one executive stated about a talented employee, "We worked hard to get her here, now we need to do everything we can to keep her."

Mentoring Is a Leadership Development Tool

As mentoring programs are implemented and expanded, organizations find that they are improving the leadership skills of a broader spectrum of their employees. Mentors act as leaders, protégé/mentees mature into leaders and leadership contributes to the health of the entire organization. Sometimes mentors comment that they were reluctant to begin the process but soon realized that they were learning as much or more than their protégé/mentees. They often learn about themselves, the organization and most often, acquire a new awareness about the experience of others.

Mentoring Is a Tool for Addressing Diversity

Formal mentoring programs and informal mentoring have been around for hundreds of years. The difference today is that employees—especially those who have been historically disenfranchised and not been part of internal "power" structures—now are able to learn and grow within their organizations. Mentoring expert David A. Thomas, in his book *Breaking Through: The Making of Minority Executives in Corporate America*, as well as the recent Catalyst study on the advancement of women support this emphatically.

Mentoring has become a major factor in an organization's ability to glean talent from their employees. Solid mentoring relationships have become a tool to assist employees so they can "hit the ground running," prepared to handle challenges, and respond when the opportunity arises. In addition, today's employees aren't willing to spend years "earning" their right for advancement. They want to know the ropes now or they will leave to go where opportunities await them.

Not only do mentoring programs look at career development and day-to-day success, but highly successful mentoring relationships develop the emotional capabilities of protégé/mentees. Research, led by respected author Daniel Goleman, puts heavy emphasis on the cultivation of emotional intelligence as a competency that is essential to the development of star performers and leaders.[1]

Today, successful mentoring programs are structured and often have high visibility. No matter how structured, however, they rely on the skills and expertise of mentors who are willing to make a commitment to developing protégé/mentees, and on the commitment by protégé/mentees to participate fully in the mentoring process.

The Results of Successful Mentoring Programs Are Compelling

- ▸ Increased ability for organizations to recruit talented and diverse employees.

- ▸ Higher retention of skilled employees.

- ▸ Increased productivity of teams.

- ▸ Heightened visibility for women and people of diverse backgrounds leading to more opportunities.

- ▸ Added respect for multicultural perspectives.

- ▸ Increased job satisfaction for mentors and protégé/mentees.

- ▸ Quicker advancement of those who are mentored.

---

[1] Goleman, Daniel, *Working with Emotional Intelligence*, Bantam, 1998.

- Evolution of new organizational leaders at all levels.

- Improved reputation outside of the organization.

Think About Metrics Now

As you start planning your mentoring program, someone will likely ask, "How will you measure success?" Recognize that there are many who are skeptical about mentoring programs, especially when employees are asked to take time away from their jobs or their team, budget dollars are requested and employees are not sure about what's in it for them. They need proof that mentoring is valuable to the organization. The earlier you understand the specific concerns of your organization, the easier it will be for you to collect the data that will determine your measurement strategy. Keep in mind that you will need data that is both qualitative and quantitative. So start a file or journal of anecdotal comments from the beginning. We will talk about how to use them in Chapter Ten.

Ten Questions to Ask Before You Begin

Although the actual steps in any process depend on the practices and systems of your company, most often companies ask questions of themselves and their leadership before they begin. Here are some questions to ask before you begin:

- What are the key business drivers for a mentoring program? How could a mentoring program address these business issues?

- What is the "value added" component of this mentoring program?

- Will the program enhance, support and complement programs and competencies already in place?

- Is there any benchmark data? If not, how can you create it?

- How will we determine the cost/benefit and the return on investment (ROI)?

- What does management see as key outcomes of a mentoring program that will determine its effectiveness? What do the participants see as key outcomes?

- What are the criteria for selection of participants? Why these criteria? How do they fit into business goals?

- How will you support those who are not selected for the mentoring program so that they will feel valued? Is there a cost if you don't address this issue?

- What are your short- and long-term business objectives for the mentoring program? How will this impact program design, rollout, length of commitment and participation?

- What leadership involvement and support will there be for the program? How can you use this support when measuring success?

The successful implementation of a mentoring program requires serious consideration of these questions. Often, the answers require input from management, key stakeholders, participants, managers and the program administrator.

With the understanding of the business case for mentoring and early consideration to metrics, you are now ready to get started.

CHAPTER TWO

Lessons Learned from "Best Practices"

Mentoring is not new. In fact, its concepts date back to Greek mythology and are based on the apprentice model for many professions. Typically people have mentors or protégé/mentees at various stages of their lives and careers, frequently without an official designation. Mentors are often just people who have led the way or shed light on a time or situation. There is no fanfare, no hoopla, and sometimes they do not even recognize till years later when they look back and realize that someone along the way had been their mentor or that they had served as a mentor for an individual.

Today, however, mentoring has taken on a fresh new meaning, especially in millennium organizations. While mentoring has gone beyond the corporate world to include colleges, associations and even youth organizations, most of the energy today can still be found within corporations. Within the business world, mentoring programs are included as part of retention strategies, professional development activities and most diversity initiatives.

Organizations are making the investment of time and resources to facilitate opportunities for individuals to build relationships with others through mentoring. And in doing that, they want to see a return on their investment.

With more and more organizations striving to glean the benefits of these programs, we are seeing some outstanding examples of "best practices" emerge and there are several lessons that can be learned. What follows are the seven lessons the authors learned after compiling data on "best practices" for the past five years.

Before proceeding to the lessons, however, it's important to define how the term "best practices" is used. Here they are defined as those activities found through work with our client organizations or those we have studied, which yield outstanding results and contain elements that can be replicated in another situation. One thing we learned is that a mentoring program involves much more than a catchy name and loud publicity. We interviewed organizations that showed beautiful brochures announcing their mentoring programs but they never got past the brochure. We observed companies that brought in consultants to work with mentors or protégé/mentees before they had given thought to how the program was going to happen. One prestigious company had a complete Web-based database designed by their technical "gurus" before the program was fully planned, so the technology drove the design. You can probably guess the results.

With that said, here is an overview of the seven lessons learned. Some will be revisited as we explore them in chapters that follow. As you read these lessons, look for key elements that can be adapted or replicated in your own program.

Lesson One:
Senior Management Is Involved

In 1999, Catalyst, a national organization focusing on women in the workplace, embarked on a study to learn more about the effect of mentoring on women in the workplace. In their study they found:

> ► Mentoring amongst minorities is a significant way to break through negative stereotypes, exclusion from formal and informal networks and lack of visibility.

- 30% of women executives and 47% of women of color pointed to "lack of mentoring" as a barrier to their advancement.

- 81% of female executives saw mentors as critical to their career.

Why Senior Leaders Support Mentoring

In highly successful mentoring programs, sponsorship comes from the top of the organization. These organizations understand and recognize:

- the "war for talent."

- the bottom-line cost of recruiting and retaining employees.

- the importance of creating a learning organization.

- the benefit of "growing your own" talent.

- the need for leaders.

- the absence of developmental opportunities for women and people of color.

- the need to bring people on board quickly.

- the desire by employees to learn how to navigate their careers.

- the benefit of meaningful conversations in our knowledge-based economy.

According to the American Management Association, the cost to replace an employee who leaves is, conservatively, 30% of his or her annual salary. If the employee is highly skilled and in demand, the cost can rise to 1.5 times the annual salary.

In our "best practices," we found senior leaders who were visible champions of mentoring and readily acknowledged the powerful impact mentoring had in their own personal development. This type of endorsement signals to others taking part that mentoring is important. When senior executives act as mentors themselves, especially mentoring women or people of color, they provide evidence that the organization is truly committed to diversity.[2]

A favorite example of senior-level support came when ProGroup was facilitating a kickoff session at General Mills for a unique co-mentoring program. This remarkable program involved the senior executives in the organization who were embarking on a one-year pairing between mixed race and mixed gender co-mentors to conduct monthly dialogues. While the goal was to increase the numbers of women and people of color at the top of the organization, the purpose of the dialogues was to provide a forum for learning from each other. The program was a mandate from General Mills CEO Steve Sanger.

Sanger began with a personal commentary that positioned mentoring as a business imperative. He talked to his executives about the importance of mentoring while acknowledging time and work pressures that everyone was experiencing. (This session occurred when the merger of General Mills and Pillsbury was announced, involving everyone in attendance.) Sanger talked about the need to fully utilize the talent within the company and, in particular, the talent in the room. He emphasized that this would require removal of any barriers to communication and continued by describing what he had learned from conversations with women and people of color and their experiences in the company. Sanger admitted that he had never given serious thought to many of the issues these diverse employees considered important. The session concluded with Sanger linking mentoring to the forthcoming merger, and underscored the importance of valuing different perspectives, especially as General Mills and Pillsbury moved forward to merge their two distinct cultures into one successful enterprise.

Certainly a story like this provides a stellar example of

2 Thomas, David; Gabarro, John, *Breaking Through: The Making of Minority Executives in Corporate America*, Harvard Business School Press, 1999.

senior leadership support, especially when a CEO is talking to his or her direct reports. But time and again, we have found the absence of senior leaders to be either an oversight by program administrators or an indication that senior leaders do not understand the impact mentoring programs will have on their bottom line. Sanger's words were the support the program needed and stood as a call to action that couldn't be ignored. Many who were hoping to postpone their involvement changed their minds and signed on, met the monthly commitment and ultimately became champions of mentoring programs.

How are you planning to involve and include senior leaders in your mentoring program? Are you seeking the support of senior leaders, or do you assume they are too busy? Have you made them aware of the business reasons for supporting the program and given them specific details on how their support could impact the program's success?

Don't forget that support from direct supervisors or managers can be just as powerful. When they show support for the program by asking participants how the mentoring is going, write a letter of invitation or show recognition at the end, it goes a long way in making the participants feel like they are valued and the program is important. This is especially true for mentors who, in the beginning, may believe they will be giving more than they will be getting. Hopefully, after a successful series of interactions mentors will see the benefit for themselves as well.

Lesson Two:
There Is a Well-thought-out Plan

With companies sponsoring mentoring programs, looking for results and evaluating the benefits of the activities surrounding mentoring, it becomes even more critical that a structure and format be established for any size roll out. Whether a division is sponsoring the mentoring or a department, clarity around the structure and expectations creates a model for success. Even informal mentoring programs should have a plan of action, which could be simple guidelines for how to move forward. There is accountability built in and participants know that there will be support throughout the process. Several key factors will let participants know that their responsibility should not be taken lightly.

Administration

A program administrator is typically appointed and serves as the key contact for the program. This responsibility is part of their performance goals and not just an added task. As part of their performance review, they are rewarded for successful execution and positive results.

The program administrator is responsible for communicating the expectations for the program and oversees the entire program.

Typical Activities of the Program Administrator

- Creating a program that can be implemented successfully (keeping in mind finances, number of support staff necessary, time constraints, technological requirements, etc.).

- Interviewing and selecting participants.

- Managing the pairing process.

- Tracking progress.

- Troubleshooting.

- Acting as a resource person for questions and advice.

- Establishing and monitoring metrics.

- Creating reports.

- Acting as the spokesperson for the program.

- Generating excitement for ongoing implementation.

Realistic Timeframe

Most everyone is busy at work these days, but interestingly, busy people are usually the ones who want to get involved in mentoring programs. Because they are so busy, participants often request a nine-month to one-year commitment, since it is doable and realistic. One company that came to ProGroup for advice had a program that required a two-year commitment. They wondered why they were having trouble sustaining momentum: the first year went well, but there was less and less interest the second year. The solution for them was to shorten the program. ProGroup believes in the "let them end on a high note" theory of success. This way, the formal program ends, but there is nothing stopping them from continuing their relationship on their own.

Expect mentors and protégé/mentees to meet for approximately one to one-and-a-half hours per month. Some will extend this time by talking on the telephone or meeting informally, but the actual commitment is most desirable when participants understand the time commitment is reasonable. Established time expectations build in accountability markers. In addition, when participants know they have limited time, they use it more effectively by tackling important subjects and engaging in meaningful conversations.

Periodic Check-ins

While mentoring programs assume good intent by all parties, people can get busy and time goes by, possibly resulting in skipped meetings, unresolved problems and issues that need to be addressed. Successful mentoring programs have scheduled check-ins with the program administrator, either formal or informal, to make sure that progress is maintained. Several organizations ProGroup works with sponsor monthly gatherings where specific subjects are discussed. Through these gatherings, the learning is extended and participants have additional networking opportunities.

Something to Talk About

This element takes us back to the quality of the interactions between participants. Often, mentoring programs start off with a flourish that quickly wanes because mentors and their protégé/mentees don't have a focus to their conversations. Sometimes there is confusion about whose agenda will be addressed. Sometimes interactions start with "So how was your week? What would you like to talk about?" And sometimes the match is so poor that participants never meet again after the orientation. When the pair come from different backgrounds and cultures, there often are assumptions that one knows or doesn't know something (like the unwritten rules for success) and important things go unspoken. As ProGroup discovered this fact through focus groups with mentors and protégé/mentees of diverse cultures, we began to create structured dialogue guides for the pairs, which prompt conversations, and these have been very helpful. Whatever tool used, however, we learned that participants appreciate some guidance. It isn't enough for the mentor to say to his or her protégé/mentee, "So, what would you like to talk about today?" It is hard to measure results when the questions are this general.

Measurable Objectives

Effective mentoring programs begin with clear objectives and attainable goals that can be monitored and measured. Once established, these objectives and goals are clearly communicated to those involved before the actual rollout. All parties need to understand how their commitment to the process fits into a bigger picture and contributes to the organization.

One mentoring program in a manufacturing environment was initiated after that company's employee satisfaction survey turned up poor marks around employee morale. Factory workers indicated that they didn't feel valued, and believed their work was not valued either. Our client was concerned because many employees were going unnoticed, yet they didn't have the skills of personal effectiveness that would enable them to receive the recognition they deserved.

ProGroup partnered with this client to create *ConnectionPairs*, a structured mentoring program matching these employees with supervisors and managers (not their own) and sometimes experienced co-workers. The pairings lasted nine months and each pair used the *ConnectionPairs* dialogue guides to develop their personal effectiveness, including their communication skills.

The goal was to improve employee satisfaction, and with the baseline metrics of the employee survey, we designed a program around a goal that was measured with the following year's survey. With a successful pilot, the program branched out as those who were protégé/mentees became mentors in subsequent rounds. All, including those who had been mentors, contributed to improved employee satisfaction scores.

Today's organizations use mentoring programs to achieve measurable results related to:

- Retention/Turnover
- Career development/Advancement
- Leadership development
- Inclusion
- Productivity
- Employee involvement
- Employee satisfaction
- Knowledge management
- Diversity

Lesson Three:
The Nomination Process Is Inclusive

Often protégé/mentees have the mistaken belief that if they are selected to go through a mentoring program they are on track for quick advancement. This makes sense in light of the fact that many corporate programs have focused on employees designated as those having "high potential" for leadership. As a result, many protégé/mentees see mentoring as a prerequisite rather than an essential developmental step.

For both the mentor and protégé/mentee candidates, look beyond the "obvious choices." Try to imagine who your top 10 choices would be in both categories, then put those names aside. Next, think of 10 more individuals who didn't come to mind at first. Many times a third or fourth round of this process is necessary to "round out" the candidates and to move beyond the obvious choices.

Mentors

Successful programs conduct a broad search to find and prepare a diverse pool of mentors, adding to it often by creating a dynamic program where mentors will readily volunteer. Highly effective relationships have resulted from pairing mentors with protégé/mentees of different genders, generations, races, ethnicities and divisions. In these situations, most mentors report that they learned as much, if not more, than their protégé/mentees.

Protégé/Mentees

The most successful method for selecting protégé/mentees is by self-nomination, with an endorsement from a manger or internal champion. Often, this process yields surprising results, as individuals who would not ordinarily be selected for mentoring have opportunities to shine. "Rising stars"—the typical employees selected for mentoring programs-often express that they should not be the only candidates for mentoring programs. Since they attract attention on their own, they are often given advice and mentored without asking. These "rising stars" typically have multiple informal mentoring relationships inside and outside of the organization.

Pairings

The best pairings come when the protégé/mentee has the opportunity to select his or her mentor from several candidates, or to make suggestions of who he or she thinks would make a good mentor. Generally there is an interview conducted by the program administrator of both mentors and protégé/mentees. Also, more and more protégé/mentees are searching online databases to find a mentor, but personal conversations and interviews continue to be a fundamental requirement. Finally, pairings that are made with considerations of perceived personality style and career interest are usually the most successful.

Lesson Four:
Benefits and Rewards for Mentors Must Be Clearly Articulated

Mentoring programs reflect an organization's commitment to ongoing learning, teaching and coaching, and the rewards for participating in mentoring are numerous. Participants understand that they are making an investment in their future and the future health of the organization. This investment doesn't stop when the program ends.

When recruiting mentors, it's important to let them know that their real reward will come from developing skills in others rather than meeting a goal or receiving monetary rewards. They will get short-term personal rewards from seeing their protégé/mentees doing high-quality work and long-term benefits by seeing them advance in their careers.

Although most potential mentors understand the importance of mentoring for the organization, it's important to explain the value of mentoring for their own personal development as well. If they can't see the personal benefit, they may not want to participate. Mentors must understand that mentoring gives them a chance to reflect on their personal success factors and enhance their leadership skills. They will discover their personal strengths and examine their own potential for growth.

Finally, when mentoring programs work, protégé/mentees will move beyond their one-on-one relationship with their mentor, and everyone will benefit from these new alliances. This often involves the mentor introducing his or her protégé/mentee to others in the organization who can perhaps help them advance their careers. Often these are people the protégé/mentee would not have had access to otherwise.

Lesson Five:
Programs Are Flexible, Yet Structured

According to Kathy Kram, author of *Mentoring at Work: Developmental Relationships in Organizational Life*, "In a diverse workforce, formal mentoring programs are a necessity, because it is all too common for people to gravitate toward mentoring people just like them." In other words, even though one-size mentoring doesn't fit everyone, some degree of structure and accountability must be provided.

Some employees, for instance, need transitional mentoring as they get started in their job and launch their career; some need career navigational mentoring; and others need leadership mentoring skills. Because of each protégé/mentee's unique situation, each will need a program with a different focus. Protégé/mentees like being part of a company program, but they also want to be in control of the process and set the pace and the direction to adjust to their needs. This is a significant change from traditional mentoring programs where the mentor was in charge of the process.

Once again, the key element is the unique need of the protégé/mentee at that point in time. Whether the goal is to create a positive image of the company, help individuals see career opportunities or help them feel welcome and learn about success, the structure can be wide and varied.

Lesson Six:
Mentors and Their Protégé/Mentees Are Well-prepared for Their Roles

Successful mentoring programs start off right. Mentors are prepared to undertake the responsibility while protégé/mentees understand what to expect, what to ask for and make a commitment to participate.

Often, this preparation is done in a kickoff meeting or orientation session. (Kickoffs and orientations are covered in Chapter Eight, but for now keep in mind that programs that are successful provide more than a contracting session—they use these sessions as an opportunity to build the foundation for the program.) When participants leave, they are clear on expectations, their roles and more importantly their responsibility—and they know what a quality conversation involves.

Lesson Seven:
Mentoring Is Not About...

While learning about what mentoring entails, it is also important to be aware of what it is not. Mentoring relationships are not about:

- ▸ Job performance.
- ▸ Securing a promotion.
- ▸ Forcing a relationship.
- ▸ Gaining access to supervisors.

It is surprising how many mentoring programs are designed for these reasons. When participants hold these expectations, the program will almost always fail. Therefore, it is critical that you address these issues, so participants will not come to the program with unrealistic expectations or false hopes. After you have discussed these issues, be sure to go back and stress the benefits of mentoring.

CHAPTER THREE

Key Players

E ven though mentoring is ultimately about the one-on-one interactions between mentor and protégé/mentee, there is also a need for someone to be in charge of the mentoring program itself. Listed below are the key players needed for a successful mentoring program and a detailed description of their roles and responsibilities.

Program Sponsors

Mentoring programs must have a "champion" or sponsor to achieve maximum success. A sponsor should be an individual who is genuinely convinced of the value of the program. Program sponsors are typically in communication with decision-makers or are themselves a decision-maker and able to:

- Assess the current climate within the organization and establish the need for a mentoring program.
- Allocate a budget for the program.
- Determine the number of employees to involve.
- Adjust the "fit" of the program with overall organizational goals.
- Review program objectives to establish meaningful metrics.

Further, the program sponsor should support the objectives of the program by:

- Selecting a program administrator.
- Assisting in the planning phase.
- Approving the timeliness of a program rollout.
- Overseeing the selection of mentors and protégé/mentees and approving the pairings.
- Communicating the benefits throughout the organization.
- Consulting managers of potential participants to seek their endorsement.

The program sponsor should also address any concerns of employees, supervisors or managers when pairs meet for mentoring. For example, if a protégé/mentee requires telephone coverage while he or she meets with his or her mentor, some individuals may complain, feeling it is unfair that they have to be responsible for this extra work. The program sponsor should handle these and similar situations, making sure all employees understand the requirements and importance of the program.

When determining who will be the best program sponsor in your organization, consider the following individuals:

- A member of the management team
- A plant supervisor or manager
- A department director
- A decision-maker
- A member of the diversity task force or training committee
- An H.R. professional

Program Administrators

The program administrator is the "go to" person and often comes from the Human Resources or Training department. The program administrator should be someone who is held in high regard by employees and is very aware of any constraints or obstacles that need to be addressed to get the cooperation necessary. This person should be comfortable discussing the program with the program sponsor and keeping the sponsor informed. Successful program administrators generally have this responsibility as one of their performance goals and are recognized and rewarded for the successful implementation of the mentoring program.

The program administrator is responsible for the following:

- Act as the "host" for the program.
- Carry out the selection and pairings process.
- Notify individuals who have been selected to participate.
- Conduct or oversee the orientation session.
- Track the progress of the pairs.
- Answer questions.
- Perform the metrics at the conclusion.
- Create reports for the program sponsor.
- Assist pairs with problems.

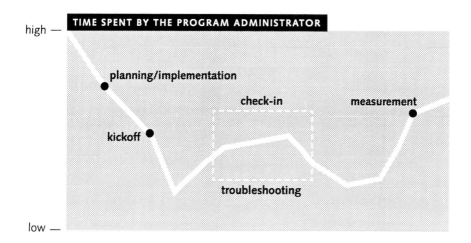

TIME SPENT BY THE PROGRAM ADMINISTRATOR

high —

planning/implementation

check-in

measurement

kickoff

troubleshooting

low —

Mentors

Mentors are individuals who have a positive history with the company and have qualities that others want to emulate. Mentors are willing to share their time and insights with their protégé/mentees for the duration of the program, and understand that these one-on-one conversations often lead to two-way learning. While each company is different, many elements of the selection process for mentors are similar. You will learn how to introduce the idea of being a mentor to a broad range of potential candidates in Chapter Seven.

Mentors can be Boomers or Gen Xers, female or male, and of any background, race or ethnicity. The pairings simply require that mentors be committed to the outcomes of the program and the goals of their protégé/mentees. However, the side benefit is the new connections that result when people are paired who may be different from each other, and they learn that what connects them is stronger than what separates them.

TEN CHARACTERISTICS OF SUCCESSFUL MENTORS

1. Aware of the organizational norms and culture.

2. Develop others through feedback and guidance.

3. Demonstrate good communication skills, both by listening and sending clear messages.

4. Act as a catalyst for change by initiating new ideas and leading others.

5. Aware of their emotions and sensitive to the emotions of others.

6. Build and maintains professional networks and relationships.

7. Would be described as "highly effective" by others.

8. Willing to share failures, as well as successes.

9. Open to individuals with different backgrounds and life experiences.

10. Demonstrate honesty and integrity.

Protégé/Mentees

Depending on the purpose of the program, a broad range of candidates are possible as protégé/mentees. Some of the greatest successes, however, have been with existing employees, often women or people of color who may have felt isolated, excluded or undervalued. These individuals develop skills and confidence from mentoring programs that enables them to demonstrate their capabilities and talents, while strengthening working relationships. Employees who hear about mentoring programs almost always want to participate.

TEN CHARACTERISTICS OF SUCCESSFUL PROTÉGÉ/MENTEES

1. Committed to the organization.

2. Know personal strengths and weaknesses.

3. Open to receive coaching

4. Take initiative to seize opportunities.

5. Conscientious about managing responsibilities and completing tasks.

6. Interested in learning the business.

7. Willing to invest time.

8. Open to listening and sharing.

9. Adaptable to new ways of thinking.

10. Demonstrate potential for growth.

Note: Chapter Seven covers the selection of mentors and protégé/mentees and explains why having criteria for selection is critical to the program's success.

CHAPTER FOUR

Designing a Program That Works for You

Each mentoring program is unique. That means each audience is different, and each approach must be tailored to meet a diverse set of needs. These different needs can be divided into three stages: transitional, navigational or leadership.

Stages of Mentoring Programs

Stage One can be described as *transitional*. This is the critical stage at the beginning of a career as a new hire, or what someone transferred into a new job or a new member of a group experiences. This is when individuals spend most of their time trying to learn their job or role and get comfortable in the organization. For those who are "different" for whatever reason, this is when they are deciding whether or not the organization is right for them. At this stage it is hard for them to find a mentor because they often don't know anyone, have low self-esteem or have ineffective interpersonal skills.

Transitional mentoring is important. The sooner individuals feel they are an important part of the organization, the sooner they will become contributing members. Typically the purpose of these programs is to improve personal effectiveness and increase organizational knowledge. Individuals, particularly people of color, find valuable developmental support in the form of advice, feedback, friendship and information-sharing from people who might not be on the fast track or senior, but who understand the corporation.

There are transitional mentoring programs with dedicated time for conversations, as well as those with loosely formed "buddy" systems. Certain peer relationships can also provide vital support for making individuals stronger protégé/mentee candidates in the future. The importance of transitional mentoring is to assure that individuals will become effective participants in the organizational community and not become isolated or excluded.

Stage Two is what most people think of when they hear the term "mentoring program." These programs address the career journey and are called *navigational*. In the past, many organizations used this form of mentoring to prepare high potential individuals for advancement.

While navigational mentoring continues, we see it falling into the diversity arena. When organizations begin exploring why they have high turnover amongst women and people of color they usually learn that it is because these individuals do not see opportunities for themselves. (In many organizations, individuals can't see opportunities because they don't exist.) Mentoring then becomes the strategy of choice used to bring those previously excluded into the fold.

ProGroup has worked with organizations to help design programs specifically for women or people of color. Some include them as part of their development programs, as is the case with one organization that has formed a multi-faceted "Women Achievers" program which pairs women mentors with women protégé/mentees. Navigational mentoring programs are often very visible with many people watching to see if they deliver results.

Pilot navigational programs can be a valuable way to test the waters, find areas that need improvement and get a feel for how successful a formal program might be. (A pilot usually involves running the program for three to six months before another is started.) Pilots can also be an excellent way to get additional support for a formal mentoring program, since you have identified problem areas in advance and therefore can avoid them before devoting time and money towards a comprehensive program.

Stage Three programs are designed to groom leaders. *Leadership* mentoring focuses on those who have been identified as potential "executive" material. Often they are people of color or women who are seen as individuals who have the capability to break through the "glass ceiling." These programs focus on networking and sponsorship, and are generally less formal. Leadership programs generally follow an intense interview and selection process where matching is done carefully.

Strong leaders, whether they are in the mentor or protégé/mentee role, have an insatiable curiosity about people, ideas and processes which enables them to envision possibilities. They enjoy mentoring situations because they can act as both teachers and students. When acting as a mentor, these leaders benefit from dialogues with their protégé/mentee and protégé/mentees gain valuable insights as well. Sometimes that means the opportunity for protégé/mentees to sit in on meetings in order to observe the business from a different angle and watch decision-making processes.

Questions to Consider

Instead of giving prescriptive answers as to how to design a program, it is more effective to look at the nuts and bolts of a standard mentoring program. From our best practices research we found certain elements that are typically involved in implementing a program. We also uncovered key questions that if asked and answered will help you determine the elements of a program that is right for your organization.

The following section outlines the most common steps involved in implementing a mentoring program, along with questions designed to help you think about your own program. It is likely these questions will generate additional question for you to consider. These steps represent a standard process, and the questions a traditional way of thinking. Don't let this stop you from incorporating new ways of thinking into the process so that you will create the best mentoring program possible for your organization.

After going through the list, ask yourself, "What could go wrong?" As always, there will be unanticipated problems, but trying to anticipate them before they happen will help you manage the overall program.

Before you tackle the questions, get in the right frame of mind. The approach described here is not advocating grandiose structures and layers of "administrivia." Our focus is on the participants and the value mentoring holds for them as well as the organization. Without a doubt, some formal structure is needed to validate the program, give it credibility and keep it inclusive to deliver the desired results, but how much structure is up to you.

Below are factors to keep in mind and questions to ask yourself as you begin planning.

- *Set up reasonable expectations that work within the parameters you were given.* What is realistic with the resources you have and the time frame?

- *Identify the support you have, the support you will need and the likelihood of getting it.* Who can you count on? Who are the champions for the program?

- *Set a launch date and work backwards when planning.* If the launch date is set for you, then go back to the beginning.

- *Don't "reinvent the wheel."* Are there pre-existing programs or tools that have already been created or people who can make implementation easier?

- *Seize the "white spaces" which are areas where you can make decisions on your own and move forward.* Will it be easier and quicker to ask for forgiveness than permission?

- *Recognize the "black spaces" which are the areas where you will need approvals and sign-offs.* Are there areas that are particularly sensitive for your company?

- *Ask others to give you feedback, including co-workers of diverse backgrounds and cultures.* Do you sometimes react to feedback as if it were criticism? If so, re-evaluate your response, and treat feedback, whether positive or negative, as a gift.

With the above factors in mind, you are ready to review the standard steps for implementing a mentoring program.

Step One
Determine and clarify the objectives of the program

1. What does management expect to achieve?

2. What business issues are linked to the success of the program?

3. How will the program be measured for success?

4. What objectives can be articulated that will help determine the audience and the design of the program?

5. Can you describe the program, its purpose and objectives in 25 words or less?

6. Is there an outcome that has been overlooked? If so, how will you incorporate it into the program?

Step Two

Determine the program structure

1. Is the program transitional, navigational or leadership mentoring?

2. Who is the audience? New hires? Career professionals? Leaders? Women? People of color?

3. What are they willing to give?
   What are they expecting to get?

4. How formal does the program need to be?

5. What is the duration of the program?
   What is reasonable?

6. How often do you expect partners to meet?
   For how long?

7. What is realistic in terms of administrative support and time frames?

8. Is a pilot program needed before a bigger rollout?

9. What will you call the program?

10. Is there any need to be innovative in the program design to adjust to the needs of the audience or organizational parameters?

11. Is there enough emphasis on what happens between the participants to enhance the quality of the interactions?

12. What are the administrative needs for monitoring progress, reporting to management, pre- and post-metrics?

Step Three

Determine your organization's ground rules

1. Who is eligible? Who is not?

2. Will there be restrictions on what happens in this program? For example, are pairs expected to meet on personal time or are they given permission to meet during work time? Will they meet off-site? If so, should they be allowed to use a company credit card to pay for lunch?

3. How much latitude do the pairs have with the program? For example, is a telephone conversation or e-mail chat considered a meeting?

4. What resources within the organization can be used?

5. How much leeway is there to include new ways of thinking? Can the pairs divert from the program objectives? Can they change the rules in any way?

Step Four

Select mentors and protégé/mentees

1. What is the criteria for selection?

2. Are there special groups to approach and encourage participation?

3. How will the selection process address the expected outcomes for the program?

4. How will you make this an inclusive process?

5. How will you recruit individuals of diverse backgrounds to participate?

6. How will you promote and encourage participation?

7. Are you broadening your pool or are you tapping individuals who are always asked to participate in special programs?

Step Five
Determine the pairs

1. Will the program sponsor determine the pairs? Using what criteria?

2. How will the candidates be involved in the pairing?

3. How will the pairings contribute to achieving your program objectives?

Step Six
Notify managers and supervisors

1. How will you notify managers and supervisors to garner their support?
2. Who is the best person to communicate the message?
3. What do you expect in terms of their support?
4. What can participants in the program expect from their managers?
5. How will you inform managers about the participant's performance at the end of the program?

Step Seven
Notify the pairs

1. How and when will you inform the pairs of their selection and pairing?
2. What will you tell them about their partner?
3. What other information will you provide?
4. What do you expect them to do next?
5. What should they begin to prepare?
6. Will participants sign a formal contract before the kickoff/orientation?

Step Eight

Conduct the kickoff/orientation session

1. Who will conduct the kickoff?
   How long will it be? When? Where?

2. Who will represent the organization and endorse the event and program?

3. What are the expectations for the kickoff/orientation?

4. What will the agenda be?
   What do participants need to know?

Step Nine

Check-ins

1. How often will you check in on the pairs?

2. How will you conduct check-ins?
   In a formal meeting, by telephone, e-mail, survey or other means of communication?

3. If you encounter problems, what will you do?

Step Ten

Conduct a rewards and recognition ceremony

1. How will you formally conclude the program?

2. How will you acknowledge and reward the mentors and protégé/mentees for their participation?

Things to Keep in Mind

Answering these questions will help you implement a mentoring program, but it does not guarantee success. Many programs have failed even with careful planning. Why? Because no consideration was given to what happens once the pairs are meeting on their own. This brings us back to our fundamental belief that the quality of the interaction between mentors and their protégé/mentees determines the value of the program. In order for the mentoring to be successful, there must be a focus to their encounters so that the time they spend is worthwhile and takes them into dialogues that produce meaningful results.

CHAPTER FIVE

Sample Program Designs

By exploring various types of mentoring programs, we discovered that there were several options that both appealed to individuals and met the desired outcomes of the organizations. The main determining factor stems from the amount of flexibility and accountability the organization desires in their mentoring program.

The key to success with structured mentoring programs is that they are able to maintain their structure, yet allow for flexibility so that participants feel they have control of the process. Below are sample program designs that are flexible and contribute to success:

- **Traditional mentoring** where one individual is assigned a mentor.

- **Group mentoring** where two to four protégé/ mentees are mentored by one mentor.

- **Multiple mentoring** where a person may have several mentors to turn to, each mentor bringing a different perspective.

- **Focused programs** such as those designated for women, people of color or a specialized professional group, like engineers or lawyers.

- **Co-mentoring** where level-to-level mentoring takes place.

There are also programs that have similarities to mentoring programs, but are different in that they use unique approaches to prepare employees for future success. These approaches include:

- *Reverse Mentoring.* Reverse mentoring currently can be found in pairings of a technical expert with a protégé/mentee. Typically the mentor is younger than his or her protégé/mentee. Although this arrangement can be beneficial, sometimes relationship issues due to the age difference occur when using this method.

- *Groundhog Job Shadowing Day.* On February 2 (Groundhog Day), employees are paired with someone they want to shadow to learn about the job and conduct dialogues over lunch.

- *Employee Loan Programs.* Here an individual works in another department or division under the guidance of a mentor for a period of time to learn another aspect of the business.

- *Cross-company Mentoring.* An example of cross-company mentoring is when women work with women of similar positions in other organizations.

- *New Hire "Buddies."* These are programs designed to provide support for those who have just entered an organization or department.

- *Recruitment Contacts.* These partnerships begin before an applicant even accepts a job. Applicants receive a call from an internal "buddy" who will answer questions through the interview process. This is especially helpful when a job requires relocation to a new community. These relationships tend to continue through the hiring process and then in the early stages of orientation.

- *Accelerated Mentoring Programs.* Accelerated mentoring programs are used in limited situations and appeal to Gen X employees. These programs help talented employees become "insiders" quickly as the protégé/mentees are generally paired with someone in a high position in the organization and involves a very short-term commitment. This occurs most often in high-tech industries or fast-paced sales operations.

- *Distance Mentoring.* Distance mentoring relationships are conducted primarily by telephone or e-mail. Since the distance affects the cohesion of the mentoring, it is important to work to find some "face time" to meet either through interactive video or scheduled meetings.

What follows are some sample mentoring designs for you to think about as you determine what will work best for you.

Dedicated Time

This format was developed by ProGroup for a manufacturing client. This client established a mentoring program that encouraged employees who were often overlooked to improve their personal effectiveness and become leaders in the plants. This transitional mentoring program included employees who were accustomed to the organization's training format and enjoyed a more structured learning environment.

Another goal was to rollout the program several times, replicating it by using mentors more than once and moving protégé/mentees into the role of mentor in subsequent rounds. Since participants were given time off from the factory line for mentoring, some for the first time, the organization felt it wanted to keep a tighter hold on the interactions. Participants were encouraged to meet outside of the established time, but were required to attend the mentoring sessions as scheduled. Each session ended with an interim activity that was reviewed at the start of the following session.

This format includes the option of having a facilitator, or a host, who greets the participants and gets them started. This person ultimately becomes a coach to the pairs as they go through the process.

For this particular manufacturing client, mentors were very new to the mentoring process and some felt uncomfortable. Therefore the facilitator spent 15 minutes with the mentors as a group to check-in before their protégé/mentees joined them. After five weeks, these check-ins were not necessary.

Description of a Dedicated Time Format

- Starts with a kickoff/orientation event to introduce pairs to the program and provide an opportunity for them to learn about their roles and responsibilities. The orientation session generally includes two hours with the mentors alone and two hours with the protégé/mentees alone. This is followed by a lunch together and concludes with a two-hour joint session. (Read Chapter Eight for further information on conducting kickoff/orientation sessions.)

- Specific time is scheduled on a regular basis for the pairs to meet.

- A facilitator or host convenes the large group and focuses their attention on a topic for conversation. In the case of ProGroup's dialogue guide *ConnectionPairs*, the topics cover personal effectiveness, building relationships, handling conflict, networking and work/life balance. Following an introduction, the pairs move to private conversations for approximately an hour and a half.

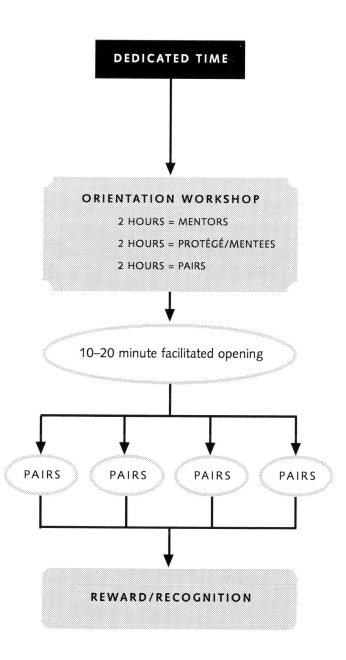

DEDICATED TIME

ORIENTATION WORKSHOP

2 HOURS = MENTORS

2 HOURS = PROTÉGÉ/MENTEES

2 HOURS = PAIRS

10–20 minute facilitated opening

PAIRS   PAIRS   PAIRS   PAIRS

REWARD/RECOGNITION

Advantages of the Dedicated Time Format

- A strong sense of community develops for the group.

- The organization is able to control and monitor the progress.

- There is a starting place for conversations with the focus on specific topics.

- Long-range plans are possible because an ending date is clear.

- The ability for protégé/mentees to move into the role of mentor for the next round is increased due to the utilization of a facilitator or coach.

- It promotes the concept of a learning organization.

Disadvantages of the Dedicated Time Format

- A suitable location must be found where pairs can hear each other and not others.

- Often distance and room scheduling becomes problematic.

- A common meeting time may not be convenient.

- It lacks flexibility for individual needs.

Things to Think About When Establishing a Dedicated Time Format

- Establish a schedule of dates and meeting times for the duration of the program.

- Expect that not everyone will be available for each of the meetings.

- Secure adequate meeting space or technological equipment for the duration of the program before the program begins.

- If a facilitator or host is used, be sure they understand their role. They are not in a training situation where they are teaching and others are learning, but rather are facilitating the mentoring process.

Flexible Time

Flexible time is the traditional format used by most organizations. The sponsoring parties get the pairs together, but then they are on their own to schedule meeting times. Often, the degree of flexibility—or lack of it—corresponds to the degree of effectiveness of the program. Left up to busy people, flexibility sometimes is interpreted as "whenever it fits into my schedule." In spite of the best of intentions, "whenever" in practical terms can mean "never." Many protégé/mentees will praise their mentors and say, "My mentor was there when I needed them," but this is not enough. A genuine commitment is needed and both parties must understand that mentoring is more than occasional friendly advice. Mentors need to be available on a proactive rather than reactive basis, and even with a flexible format, some structure is necessary, even if that structure is simply the expectation that monthly conversations will occur.

Description of the Flexible Time Format
Flexible time mentoring is started with a kickoff event to introduce pairs to the program. After the first session, pairs are asked to meet on a regular basis over a set period of time (usually ranging from nine to 18 months). Pairs are responsible for continuing their meetings, with periodic check-ins from the program administrator. A reward and recognition ceremony during the final week generally completes the program.

Advantages of the Flexible Time Format

- Pairs can schedule time and place according to their schedules.

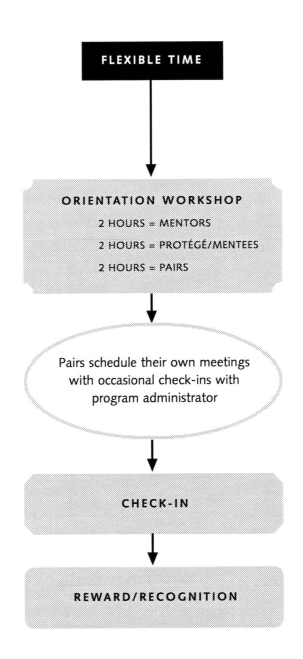

FLEXIBLE TIME

ORIENTATION WORKSHOP

2 HOURS = MENTORS

2 HOURS = PROTÉGÉ/MENTEES

2 HOURS = PAIRS

Pairs schedule their own meetings with occasional check-ins with program administrator

CHECK-IN

REWARD/RECOGNITION

- Pairs are in charge of their program.
- Pairs feel ownership in the program.
- Face-to-face meetings aren't essential.

Disadvantages of the Flexible Time Format

- Without a set time, other commitments may take priority.
- If meetings are missed, the program has less of an impact.
- Administration and monitoring are more difficult.
- One or both parties can lose interest.

Things to Think About with a Flexible Time Format

- A time frame needs to be established for the conclusion of the program.
- The program administrator needs to check in with pairs on a periodic basis to monitor the progress.
- The program administrator needs to speak to each participant's manager or supervisor to ask for support as the process continues.
- The program administrator needs to suggest meeting rooms or locations where pairs can meet.
- The program administrator needs to establish a rewards and recognition ceremony.

Distance Mentoring

As companies become more global, many are trying to implement distance mentoring electronically. Whether through e-mail, Web cam or long distance there are many benefits to using technology for communication and mentoring. While distance mentoring would seem like a valuable tool, it is still new and the impact hasn't been clearly measured. However, for job-specific mentoring and even some professional development electronic communication has proven to be very valuable. The primary limitation of distance mentoring is that it is more difficult to share sensitive or personal information. Since confidentiality is a critical element of mentoring, and Intranet e-mails are often subject for review, protégé/mentees may have concerns that their e-mail communication will not remain private. Also, it is nearly impossible to build a close rapport via electronic communication.

Description of Distance Mentoring

- Pairs and virtual teams manage their conversations electronically.

- Program materials and introductory information are provided through e-mail or downloaded from the company's Intranet or the Internet.

- Administrators keep track of sessions.

- Multiple mentors and protégé/mentees can be linked.

- Some are designed like chat lines for instant messaging; others are e-mail-based.

Advantages of Distance Mentoring

- Protégé/mentees can be mentored from long distances and matches that could otherwise not be possible, are possible.

- It leverages and reinforces the use of existing technological resources.

- The cost is minimal.

- Anytime, any day mentoring can take place.

- Mentoring conversations are on an as-needed basis.

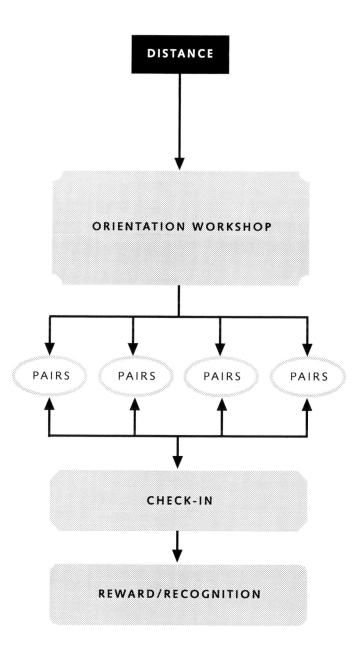

- Tracking and administrating is easier.
- Since younger employees are usually comfortable with electronic communication, it often appeals to them.

Disadvantages of Distance Mentoring

- There is a loss of personal contact.
- Often employees do not engage as freely due to the perceived lack of confidentiality.
- It can be difficult to communicate emotional issues in writing.
- The electronic format can be cumbersome, especially for those who have limited typing skills or don't feel they have adequate writing skills.
- Conversations are focused and don't provide the opportunity to explore new paths.
- Mentors may not be "techno savvy" and are not as comfortable with this method of communication.
- It works better for some desired outcomes over others. For example, it would not work well for a protégé/mentee who was trying to learn the nuances of a leadership style from a role model.

Things to Think About

The distance mentoring format adds an additional layer to the planning process, since you need to work closely with your Information Technology team. These professionals will play a key role in the success of a distance mentoring program, and it is important to get them on board early. Before you begin a distance mentoring program, be sure to consider the following questions with your technology experts:

- Will the organization's existing computer system support the day-to-day communication needs of pairs (e.g., is e-mail readily available, do all mentoring pairs have access to computers and software, are all employees on the same or compatible platforms)?

- Is there a "Help Line" participants can call or is similar support available?

- What are the organization's policies regarding the confidentiality of e-mail?

- What level of confidentiality can be assured, if any?

- Does the technology for video conferencing exist? Are there additional charges for its use?

- Is there a company-wide Intranet that can host program information and updates?

- Are technology experts from your IT team available to assist as needed, or should an external resource be used?

Group Mentoring

Description of the Group Time Format

In group time mentoring, a single mentor is matched with several protégé/mentees. Similar to the other formats, a large group orientation/kickoff session is strongly recommended. Special attention is focused on group communication dynamics and individual responsibilities for accountability and support of the group process. The group time mentoring process relies heavily on a strong mentor who assures the needs of all members of the group are being met. Typically no more than four protégé/mentees are paired with a single mentor.

Advantages of the Group Time Format

The group time format reinforces the idea of teamwork and shared use of resources (a single mentor, combined meeting times, less concern with available meeting space, etc.) and is often an attractive option for programs with limited budgets and time. Ideally, the interaction among group members will spark creativity and energy that will flow over to other workplace interactions, creating an environment of productivity and focus throughout the organization.

Disadvantages of the Group Time Format

Unfortunately group time format is often used by organizations to "weed-out" protégé/mentees who are considered to be not serious about the program. The intent is to start with three or four protégé/mentees but end up with one or two. The "star performers" will identify themselves, it is thought, by being motivated to navigate the group process by attending meetings and being prepared. Too often, the process itself frustrates those who would benefit most from mentoring and many become alienated by rigid group structure, dysfunctional group dynamics or scheduling conflicts that are out of their control.

Things to Think About

If you are considering a group mentoring format, ask yourself the following:

- ▸ Why does this format seem attractive?
  Have you thought out the pros and cons to this format?

- ▸ Do you have mentors who have the skills to be dynamic group facilitators?

- ▸ Where and when will they meet?

- ▸ What added value will the group process bring to your organization—tying together diverse groups, unifying those separated by geographic distance or the sharing of professional expertise?

- ▸ How will you measure the success of the mentoring?

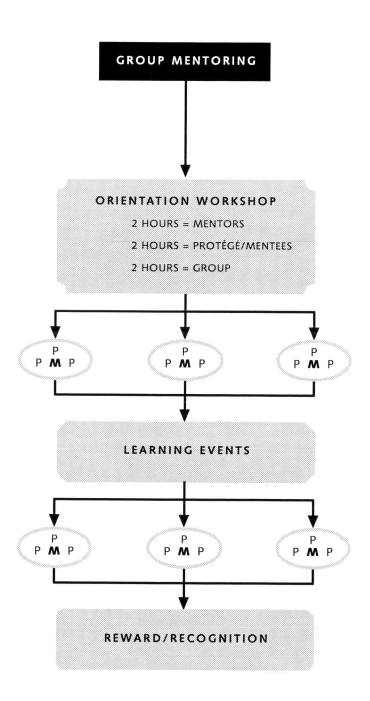

GROUP MENTORING

ORIENTATION WORKSHOP

2 HOURS = MENTORS

2 HOURS = PROTÉGÉ/MENTEES

2 HOURS = GROUP

P
P **M** P

P
P **M** P

P
P **M** P

LEARNING EVENTS

P
P **M** P

P
P **M** P

P
P **M** P

REWARD/RECOGNITION

Things to Keep in Mind

There are many advantages and disadvantages to each of the formats we have explored. After reviewing these different formats, you may discover that a hybrid of several options seems like the best solution for your organization.

As you proceed, keep in mind that your program should be easy to explain and easy to implement. Build in check-ins along the way to make sure that you will yield the results you desire. As you check in, be sure to ask about the quality of the mentoring, not just about the structure of the program.

If this is the case, be sure to follow the suggestions described previously for exploring the many aspects of your model in order to strengthen your credibility as the program administrator. Finally, always remember, there are no "right" answers, only creative solutions to be discovered!

CHAPTER SIX

Application and Nomination Process

As stated earlier, the "value added" benefits of a mentoring program are derived from an open and inclusive process for determining who will participate in the program.

Typical corporate "silos" often found in organizations create boundaries which can discourage otherwise motivated employees from learning, excelling and moving beyond their current position. Today's young motivated employees are continually looking for ways to build their résumés. These employees often are seeking cross-functional/division mentoring opportunities in order to improve their skills and keep themselves marketable. Opportunities to work with a mentor from another division may mean the difference between a talented employee staying with the company or leaving to pursue better opportunities.

"Up and coming" employees often are not noticed or nurtured in the same intentional manner as those deemed the "best and brightest." Unfortunately, these individuals are the ones who typically don't fit the organization's "model for success" and often leave quietly to go to other organizations where they believe they will be valued.

Some employees, including women and people of color, will volunteer for mentoring programs, believing they will provide the interactions they need in order to be successful. According to our interviews (and supported by the work of David A. Thomas), opportunities to work with an internal mentor are seen as valuable opportunities; however, when these protégé/mentees are paired with a mentor of a different race or gender there is often a degree of discomfort for both parties. These relationships seldom result in the close interpersonal bonds encouraged between mentor and protégé/mentee. (Typically, women and people of color find their real support from mentors outside of their current organization. These mentors can be across companies or industries, or within their network groups.)[3]

As you consider the goals of your program, you will be able to determine how broad a net is cast for participants. For example, if you are involved in *transitional* mentoring, you should consider employees who have worked less than two years in the organization or department as protégé/mentee candidates. In transitional mentoring, mentors can be peers, other managers and/or supervisors.

Some organizations have used their affinity networks to create informal mentoring programs and to find mentors and protégé/mentees for transitional programs. Because these affinity groups are created to provide support for homogeneous groups of employees, as well as keep the organization apprised of issues that are important to the group, they become a valuable intra-organizational resource for employees. For example, individuals from an African-American affinity group or a Gay-Lesbian employee network might provide valuable networking and informal mentoring for a new individual.

If your program is designed as *navigational,* then mentors and protégé/mentees are determined by specific selection criteria and a formal interview process. Many employees will want to be part of these programs, so it is important that selection criteria is made public and followed. Rather than rejecting employees who are interested, consider ways to do additional pairings, even if the program begins months in the future. Typically, more employees will want a mentor than volunteer to be a mentor.

---

[3] Thomas, David; Gabarro, John, *Breaking Through: The Making of Minority Executives in Corporate America,* Harvard Business School Press, 1999.

Leadership programs are selective, requiring careful consideration when selecting and matching pairs. Same race and gender mentoring at this level is very effective, but women and people of color report advantages to having anyone as a mentor at this level as long as there is honest dialogue about their differences. When this happens they can begin to build a comfortable and trusting relationship.

Seeking Mentors and Protégé/Mentees

Often the most important "tool" in the selection process is one-on-one conversations with individuals to get them interested in mentoring programs. Use these conversations to share the following information:

- ► Explain the program to the person you are contacting.

- ► Share if nominations will be requested from the entire company or if you are personally selecting mentor and protégé/mentee candidates.

- ► Provide them with the goals of the program, the time commitment required and the value of the program, both to them and the organization.

- ► Share why you believe they would be an excellent mentor or protégé/mentee.

- ► Ask if they would be interested in participating in such a program.

- ► Ask if they can recommend others who might be interested in participating.

- ► Share your timeline with them.

- ► Provide them with a deadline for when you will contact them for their decision (typically no more than one week) and the start date of the program (typically no more than two to four weeks after contacting them).

Frequently Asked Questions

As a program sponsor or administrator, you will also serve as a resource person. Below is a list of frequently asked questions and responses to assist you as you work with the participants in your mentoring program.

Q. *What's in it for me?*
A. An opportunity to contribute, grow professionally and a chance to take the spotlight and demonstrate your capabilities.

Q. *What if my job gets busy and I have time pressures?*
A. This program has been deemed a priority by management and while flexibility is possible, a commitment to participate fully is expected.

Q. *What will my manager and supervisor think?*
A. Your manager will be notified and informed that their support is needed in order for the program to work.

Q. *Who will cover for me while I'm gone?*
A. What arrangements are needed?
Who can cover for you? We'll work with your manager to make sure that you are covered.

Q. *What if I don't get along with my protégé/mentee? Mentor?*
A. The program administrator will be available to handle problems if they occur.

The Application Process

Each organization has different ways of implementing new processes, and it is important to be aware of them when implementing your mentoring program. Below are suggestions for creating your own application process.

Notify potential participants of the mentoring program. State the goals and objectives of the program clearly and enthusiastically, and describe the unique characteristics of the candidates you are seeking. Be sure to include the benefits individuals can expect by participating. Let these potential participants know the names of senior executives and others who are supporting the program. It is also helpful to present the information so the potential participants clearly understand that they have been singled out because the company recognizes their potential. This should not be seen as another responsibility, but as a valuable opportunity.

- Create appropriate information packets and application materials. Make it easy for participants to apply, but be sure you get any information you need to keep the program moving forward. (See samples in the Appendix.)

- Make calls to explain the program to those who need additional encouragement or information.

- Distribute application materials—include deadlines and expectations for participating in the program—and be sure to allow candidates at least one to two weeks to complete the applications and return them to you. (See Appendix for sample letters.)

- Plan to check in with candidates once or twice during the application process to assure that all materials are received on time. (This can be a simple reminder sent via e-mail.)

- Once an application is received, send a pre-interview questionnaire to be completed and returned. The answers provided on this question-naire will help prepare for an interview with the candidates. (See Appendix for Pre-Interview Questionnaire.)

▸ Decide who will be conducting the interviews. If it will be a team interview, be sure to clarify the selection criteria so all are working from the same premise.

CHAPTER SEVEN

Selecting and Pairing Mentors and Protégé/Mentees

The selection process typically begins with the program sponsor and administrator carefully considering the goals of the program. Here is where the business case for your mentoring program comes into play again. If the selection and pairing are done in consideration of the business issues the program is addressing, then the rationale for who is involved is clear. That means that you have specific criteria for selecting some individuals over others. It also will make the pairings easier and it will be easier to encourage certain individuals to participate. In other words, this mentoring program is based on an organizational goal that may mean some new ways of thinking are necessary.

There are three fundamental principles for selecting mentors and protégé/mentees.

1. *Establish criteria for selection of participants based on the business drivers behind your mentoring program.* Be prepared to answer: Why them? Why not me?

2. *Select individuals who have something to contribute to the organization and will benefit from the mentoring process, either as a mentor or a protégé/mentee.* You are making an investment of time and resources in these employees. What is the benefit to them? To the organization?

3. *Think about inclusivity versus exclusivity as you seek individuals to be both mentors and protégé/mentees.* Go beyond those that "come to mind."

Determine the Process for Selection

The program sponsor and program administrator should determine whether the selection process will be open or closed.

An *open process* will involve the nomination of candidates from a large pool of employees, including those employees who self-nominate after learning about the benefits of the program. They are generally interviewed to determine their goals and objectives for the mentoring experience and their desired characteristics in a partner.

Protégé/mentees may suggest their own mentor based on their personal goals and objectives. They may have identified these mentor candidates as "good developers of people" by working on teams or special projects with them, and see these individuals as good developmental mentors.

One suggestion when developing your mentoring program is to put together an online database of potential mentors. Protégé/mentees can then go online and look for mentors who have qualities that match their objectives. After selecting two or three possibilities, they conduct face-to-face interviews and ultimately select a mentor.

A *closed process* involves recommendations of the candidates for mentors and protégé/mentees from managers or team leaders. Generally, this list of candidates is based on criteria related to the desired outcomes of the program. For example, if an organization notices that women tend to leave after two to three years of employment, they might create a program designed to address retention of women. Or, your organization may have high turnover in a particular group, talent needs (such as a lack of engineers) or you may have a poor image as an employer. All these issues will determine who you look for as participants in the program.

Regardless of the method chosen, be sure to consider those who may not be the first to "come to mind." Often the best mentor and protégé/mentee candidates are not the individuals who are included on the first or second list. They may have mentor potential with skills that are untapped, or they may be protégé/mentee candidates who have skills yet to be developed.

The selection process is difficult, because it is likely someone will feel excluded—and some may be very vocal about their feelings. For example, white males may ask, "What about me? I never had an opportunity to work with a mentor." These situations require tact and delicacy. While many white males have been part of the informal mentoring process, they often don't recognize it. Perhaps they have been groomed by a boss, or are part of the exclusive "club" and learn the unspoken "rules" for success, for example, while socializing on the golf course.

Because of the potential for some to feel excluded, it's important to prepare answers to these questions in advance, know that some individuals may be unhappy and keep your program focused on your organizational goals. Also, be sure to carefully consider how your program is communicated and marketed. Keep in mind that in many organizations, there were no formal mentoring programs in existence before "diversity" became a popular term. There may be a tendency to believe that mentoring is for "those" people and not for the good of the organization. Many organizations have found that it is important to do a good job of diversity education before embarking on any mentoring program so that individuals understand the elements of an inclusive culture.

Selecting Mentors

The pool for mentors generally includes those who volunteer or have been identified as good role models and developers of people. Many individuals are unaware of their potential as mentors. They may have never thought of themselves as mentor material, and may need encouragement before they agree to participate. It's important to provide mentors with a clear under-

TEN CHARACTERISTICS OF MENTORS	LOW HIGH
1. Aware of the organizational norms and culture.	1 5
2. Develops others through feedback and guidance.	1 5
3. Demonstrates good communication skills, both by listening and sending clear messages.	1 5
4. Acts as a catalyst for change by initiating new ideas and leading others.	1 5
5. Aware of their own emotions and sensitive to the emotions of others.	1 5
6. Builds and maintains professional networks and relationships.	1 5
7. Would be described as "highly effective" by others.	1 5
8. Willing to share failures, as well as successes.	1 5
9. Open to individuals with different backgrounds and life experiences.	1 5
10. Demonstrates honesty and integrity.	1 5

standing about the commitment they will be making when discussing the mentoring process. Once they are convinced that mentoring is worthwhile, you will need to determine how best to utilize their skills and talents.

Some organizations have what is called a mentor pool. This pool contains names of mentors who have volunteered or who already were solicited and screened. As protégé/mentees are identified, they are assigned two mentor candidates from the pool. After interviewing mentors, the protégé/mentee selects one of the two as their mentor. The remaining mentor is put back in the pool until selected. The mentor pool is valuable in that it allows for an on-demand approach to mentoring which is very accommodating and timely.

Review the ten characteristics of mentors listed in the chart to the left and use these as a guide as you interview and ultimately select mentors to take part in your program.

Selecting Protégé/Mentees

Just as with the selection of mentors, your criteria for the selection of protégé/mentees must be linked to the stated outcomes of the program and the metrics for it. For example, if your goal is to increase utilization of skilled, yet often disenfranchised employees, then active recruiting must take place to encourage these employees to apply.

Nominations for candidates might come from managers as they find employees who could benefit from mentoring. In some cases, a notification is sent to managers including the selection criteria and they are asked to nominate individuals to take part in the program.

Review the ten characteristics of protégé/mentees listed on the following page and use these as a guide as you interview and ultimately select mentors to take part in your program.

TEN CHARACTERISTICS OF PROTÉGÉ/MENTEES	LOW	HIGH
1. Committed to the organization.	1 5	
2. Knows personal strengths and weaknesses.	1 5	
3. Open to receive coaching on personal and professional development.	1 5	
4. Takes initiative to seize opportunities.	1 5	
5. Conscientious about managing responsibilities and completing tasks.	1 5	
6. Interested in learning the business.	1 5	
7. Willing to invest time.	1 5	
8. Open to listening and sharing.	1 5	
9. Adaptable to new ways of thinking.	1 5	
10. Demonstrates potential for growth.	1 5	

Additional Criteria for Selection

- Years of service
- Level in the organization
- Expressed desire for professional development
- Recommended for professional development
- Performance
- Professional specialty
- Career history
- Department/division
- Functional role
- Ethnicity, gender, age, sexual orientation
- Developmental stage
- Talents or skills
- Experience outside of the organization

Remember that most matchings will work well. However, there may be some where one or both participants have created an unworkable situation. The program administrator must be prepared to offer coaching, and in many cases a graceful way for people to leave the process without feeling like failures.

Once the pairs are determined, announce them. This should be done no later than two weeks after the applications are due in order to keep the momentum going. If the process is well planned from the beginning, the announcement is seen simply as the next step and not a major event.

Pairing

Matching protégé/mentees and mentors is not an easy thing to do, and there are many questions about how to do it. It would be helpful if there was a specific formula to follow, but, unfortunately, when it comes to making matches, much is based on gut instinct.

In matching, there are primary and secondary factors to be considered. The primary factors deal with identified goals and outcomes, both personal and organizational, and the secondary factors deal with compatibility.

Primary Factors: Goals and Outcomes

These factors include the following:

- Background or experiences
- Career path
- Seniority
- Gender
- Ethnicity
- Skills
- Department, job, function
- Geographic location
- Personal goals and objectives of the program
- Previous participation in a mentoring program

These factors may play out differently in different organizations. Some may be considered in terms of similarities or differences. For example, the greatest growth opportunities may result from mentors and protégé/mentees who are from the same geographic location, while in other cases, pairs from different geographic locations who meet via distance mentoring may provide the best learning opportunities.

This primary information can be gathered through interviews with the candidates and from anecdotal information from managers and co-workers. Below are six questions to ask candidates that will help you make the matches. (Additional questions can be found in the Appendix in the Mentor/Mentee Interview Guide.)

1. What do you expect from this mentoring program?

2. What are your personal goals from this mentoring relationship?

3. What are your fears or concerns?

4. Use five words to describe the "perfect" mentor (protégé/mentee).

5. What would make this investment in time worthwhile?

6. What is the greatest "gift" a mentor (protégé/mentee) could give you?

Secondary Factors: Compatibility

Compatibility involves considering personal style issues that are examined in instruments like the Myers-Briggs Type Indicator, Learning Styles Inventory, D.I.S.C. profile and others, as well as the candidate's work history. We recommend that you ask each mentor and each protégé/mentee to complete an assessment like the one that follows. After completing the assessment, it is up to the program administrator or a designated group to determine if the matches will be successful. The column labeled "Importance in Mentoring Relationship" will provide valuable information on how much flexibility you have to take some chances in matching. Those making the matches should do their own tabulation on the "Importance to Mentoring Relationship" column and use this as additional matching criteria.

Additional Factors

One factor that is difficult to describe but is very real is the "connection" that the two parties may or may not have—in other words, the things they can identify in one another that resembles their own life experiences or aspirations. Do they see anything that reminds them of a younger or older version of themselves? If the pairings are made by an outside party, this may be difficult to assess. ProGroup encourages all new mentoring partners to spend time finding these connections as a way to increase the effectiveness of the program. If you are providing an opportunity for protégé/mentees to interview, you can be certain that this is one factor—conscious or subconscious—that is being considered.

CHARACTERISTIC	BEST DESCRIBES YOU	IMPORTANCE IN MENTORING RELATIONSHIP
Communication Style	introvert . . extrovert	high . . . . low
Interpersonal Style	task . . . . relationship	high . . . . low
Organizational Knowledge	high . . . . low	high . . . . low
Years of Service	0 . . . . 5 . . . .10+	high . . . . low
Visibility in Organization	high . . . . low	high . . . . low
Personal Style	think . . . . feel	high . . . . low
Work Style	concrete . . . abstract	high . . . . low
Learning/ Teaching Style	random . . sequential	high . . . . low
Decision-making Style	deliberate . . cautious	high . . . . low
Availability	free . . . . . scheduled	high . . . . low
Other Factors		
► Gender		high . . . . low
► Ethnicity		high . . . . low
► Age		high . . . . low

CHAPTER EIGHT

Setting the Stage for Success

Even if it appears that your mentoring program is ready to launch, it is likely there are still several details you have overlooked. Described below are the details that are often missed, some of the reasons why a program might have problems and what you can do to avoid these problems.

Notifying Managers

One of the key success factors for a mentoring program is the support it gets from managers and supervisors. Some managers are encouraging and want to keep informed of the mentoring relationship. Others may focus on the time employees take from their "real" jobs and will fail to see the bigger picture. It is possible that a manager may even become jealous of the close relationships that can develop between mentoring pairs. It is important to be aware of possible conflicts and be prepared with possible solutions.

Once the pairs are identified, the program administrator should notify managers and supervisors as early as possible so they recognize that they are valuable to the process. Managers and supervisors should understand the program goals for the organization and the participants, and should know the expectations of the program for their employees.

One way to notify managers is to have your CEO or a senior executive send a letter to managers that explains the program. Another is to invite the managers to the kickoff session. You can also include the managers in the closing session.

Orientation/Kickoff

The importance of a well-planned orientation/kickoff session cannot be stressed enough. We have chosen the words "orientation" and "kickoff" deliberately, because they must go hand in hand, if you program is to be successful.

The word "orientation" implies that when mentors and protégé/mentees leave the session, they will have all the information they need to assume their roles. The word "kickoff" suggests there will be an event that marks the commencement of the program. After attending the kickoff, mentors and protégé/mentees will know that they are involved in an important program that will make a difference for them and the organization. Both orientations and kickoffs are essential to set the stage for a successful mentoring program.

We have deliberately omitted the concept of contracting with mentoring programs, even though you may see this used in other mentoring resources. We believe that when you ask participants to sign contracts, the dynamic changes, and suddenly the mentoring program begins to sound like a business deal. It is better to think of the pairs as making a commitment to learn together and present the program this way.

Unfortunately, many kickoffs get the program off to a bad start. Often mentors and protégé/mentees meet, have refreshments and hear from the program sponsor who usually is very enthusiastic, and it ends up feeling like a high school pep fest. The mentor partners then say good-bye and, in the case of one lawyer who was to act as a mentor, left the event and hasn't talked to his protégé/mentee in six months. When asked why, the lawyer stated that it wasn't clear what the next steps should be. Neither the lawyer nor his protégé/mentee had been involved in a mentoring relationship before, got busy and didn't pursue it further.

Orientations should be spent relaying information that will help prepare partners for mentoring. During the orientation, pairs clarify their roles in the relationship and learn and

TYPICAL ROLES OF MENTORS AND PROTÉGÉ/MENTEES		
	MENTOR	PROTÉGÉ/MENTEE
Responsible for	Coaching	Learning
	Developing	Practicing
	Modeling	Questioning
	Advising	Reflecting
	Counseling	Following
	Sponsoring	Modeling
Communicates by	Demonstrating	Asking
	Participating	Exploring
	Sharing	Experiencing
	Showing	Shadowing
	Questioning	Reporting

practice quality conversations to prepare themselves to continue these conversations on a regular basis.

Don't be concerned about making the kickoff "flashy" or providing the pairs with lots of details. The most important thing you can do is explain their roles and responsibilities, talk about the expectations they have for each other and describe the nuances of conducting meaningful dialogues together. The first event should also be seen as their first meeting together and from here the process unfolds.

Here is what is recommended for a one-day orientation/kickoff:

- Consider hiring an outside facilitator who has experience with mentoring programs. By using an external consultant with mentoring experience, you will ensure that your mentoring program is off to a good start. (ProGroup is always available to conduct orientations and kickoffs.)

- Begin the day with a two-hour session with the mentors alone and two hours with the protégé/mentees alone. (ProGroup typically runs these simultaneously.) This time is used to hone in on their roles and responsibilities.

- Talk to mentors about what they want out of the mentoring relationship. Conduct candid discussions about resistance, discussing their concerns, attitudes and behaviors about working with individuals who are "different" than they are. We suggest things they can put into their "mentor toolkit" to be more effective, such as stories, examples, techniques, questions, etc. and use this to draw on for their mentoring. (ProGroup has a resource for mentors entitled *The Art of Mentoring* that contains tips and techniques for mentoring, with emphasis on how to use dialogue effectively.)

- Use your two hours with the protégé/mentees to help clarify their goals and understand their role in the relationship. As with the mentors, have an open and honest discussion about their fears, concerns and expectations.

▸ After meeting separately, bring the two groups together. Ask the pairs to sit together, then move into a discussion to learn more about the program. A program sponsor or leader should establish the organizational goals and the hopes for the program. Consider using some anonymous comments from the interviews as a way to address concerns participants might have.

▸ The next step is to conduct a mini-workshop to establish the foundation for the conversations the pairs will have when they meet.

▸ The pairs are asked to meet and conduct their first mentoring session. This includes a conversation about the "Rules for the Road" which establishes the guidelines for how they will continue. These rules include such things as who sets the meetings, where they will meet, what to do if someone must cancel, etc. At this time, they should also set the time and place for the first meeting.

If you are using ProGroup's dialogue guides, introduce the participants to the suggested topics for discussion. In most cases, this preview puts the pairs at ease because they know the agenda for their first meeting, and have time to think about the topic they will be discussing.

Check-ins

Depending on the type of mentoring program you have established, you may want to check in on the pairs on a periodic basis. One suggestion is to bring everyone back at the half-way point to reinforce the learning and allow for sharing with others in the program. Some organizations set up a quick e-mail check-in that is required monthly. Others have a sophisticated online administrative system where they can monitor the number and frequency of the meetings. The best advice is to use check-ins as a way to let the pairs know that you interested in their progress, and also as a reminder that this is a formal program, and they are expected to be meeting their end of the bargain.

Journals

Whether you use ProGroup's dialogue guides or provide a journal to each participant, it is important for mentors and protégé/mentees to document their meetings and to take notes throughout the mentoring process. While these are meant to be private and will not be collected, they do serve as a valuable tool. Protégé/mentees can use their journals to jot down key learnings and questions and can be used to capture interim thoughts to be brought back to the process. Having a journal adds another dimension to their participation in the mentoring program.

Troubleshooting

If you are a program administrator, it is important to establish yourself as the resource person for the program at the beginning of the program. Make sure pairs will be comfortable coming to you with any questions or concerns, and let them know that any personal information they share will remain confidential. (Problems most often arise when someone misses a meeting, is difficult to reach or when the pairs just aren't working.)

SYMPTOM	ACTION
Mentor and protégé/mentee are not a good fit.	Speak to program administrator. Mediate to see if there is a particular problem. Look for another option.
The program is taking too much time.	Adjust goals and expectations.
The conversations aren't valuable.	Define a focus for each meeting.
Pairs say they need more time.	Suggest they meet outside of scheduled time or cut back on some of their dialogues.
Meetings are cancelled and rescheduled too often.	Check the commitment and reinforce the expectations.
Mentor or protégé/mentee disagrees with the process or goals.	Listen to their concerns and provide more information and educate them on the outcomes.
One party views the program as a low priority and gives limited time and energy.	Question to learn the basis for the behavior. Adjust if necessary. Find a new partner if one party is losing the opportunity to have a meaningful experience.

Rewards and Recognition

It's a major achievement to complete a nine- or 12-month mentoring program. To recognize this achievement, and put closure on the mentoring program, conduct a closing rewards and recognition session. During this session, pairs can reflect on what they have learned and gained from the relationship. At this time, they should receive a certificate of completion or a gift as a reminder that this investment of time and energy was worthwhile. We also suggest that some indication of their success be included in their personnel file.

Finally, keep in mind that each organization has its own unique way of bringing programs to a close. Will the participants be expecting a more formal "ceremony" or will a casual gathering work best? Look at how other successful programs at your organization have been concluded in the past as a guide.

CHAPTER NINE

Supporting Effective Dialogue

Throughout this book, we have discussed the importance of the quality of the interactions between participants. This is what makes the difference in the effectiveness of a mentoring program. The quality of the conversations, the openness to listening—really listening—and the willingness to share of oneself and provide honest feedback are what is at the core of the encounters between mentor and protégé/mentee.

Doing this is not easy. Most of us are more comfortable engaging in discussions where topics remain at the surface level. At other times, we listen to opinionated speakers tell us what they think, and have little opportunity to voice our own opinions. But keeping quiet, or avoiding deeper discussions won't lead to meaningful mentoring relationships, especially if the participants come from different backgrounds and cultures, life experiences or work experiences. What is effective, however, is to link the skills of dialogue with mentoring. ProGroup has done this by providing discussion topics through our dialogue guides. This way there is a focus and structure, and participants better understand their roles.

Consider a typical mentoring situation today: a senior executive is a mentor for someone who is new to the organization, a person of color or a woman, perhaps. In many cases, this mentor is part of the majority culture, which means they have had many opportunities and "privileges" that they probably aren't even aware of. Often these mentors don't realize that there is a set of unwritten rules that people need to know in order to be successful, and often they are learned the hard way. Because of this, ProGroup created workbooks that prompt dialogues around the unspoken rules for success. The results have been very positive.

It is important to think of the following as you plan to support effective dialogue between participants. First provide a suggested list of topics for conversation. These could be items taken from the interviews or topics that are predetermined because they are considered important to the organization. The topics can include suggested conversation starters (as we have included in ProGroup's dialogue guides) or they can be just a list of suggested topics.

Topics may range from personal to professional, career to organization or anywhere in between. Here are some examples:

- ▸ Your Career Journey
- ▸ Building Networks
- ▸ Increasing Visibility Within the Organization
- ▸ Qualities of a Star Performer
- ▸ Building Working Relationships
- ▸ Increasing Organizational Knowledge
- ▸ Understanding the Business
- ▸ Influencing Others
- ▸ Leadership
- ▸ Work/Life Effectiveness
- ▸ Diversity Issues

Remind the pairs that these topics are suggestions, and explain why they are important to cover. Instruct participants to use them as triggers for conversation, but remind them they are also free to:

- Expand on them.
- Add additional topics.
- Spend as much time on them as needed.
- Make sure that the personal goals of both mentor and protégé/mentee are met.

Also, use your kickoff/orientation as a place to talk about how to create effective dialogue and have the pairs practice. Remind them that they both are responsible for setting the tone so that there is free exchange of ideas.

Elements of Effective Two-way Mentoring

Both parties:

- Maintain a "safe container" for open and honest conversations.
- Voice their truth and listen to the truth of others.
- Accept the impossibility of fully understanding each other's experience while acknowledging their experience is real.
- Stay tuned to biases or assumptions that may prevent their ability to listen and empathize.
- Listen intently.
- Suspend judgments and assumptions.

Structure time for the pairs to build personal connections and talk about their goals for the program. Together they should leave knowing when and where the next meeting will be and what they might talk about, so that both parties can prepare. In a more formal program, they might report these topics to the program administrator.

CHAPTER TEN

Measuring Success

Program sponsors and administrators most likely will be responsible for measuring the results of the mentoring program. And as with any program, you can expect some analysis as to its success. Program sponsors and administrators are responsible for collecting data and interpreting it, then communicating that knowledge so it addresses the Return on Investment (ROI) of time and resources to the program.

Data comes from the periodic check-ins and anecdotal evidence that the program administrator gathers throughout the process. Much of this data will come from the personal stories that are gathered and the comments that are overheard. Gathering useful data is critical to support the goals of the program. For example, a recently promoted, mid-level African-American manager was mentored by a white male mentor. The mentor not only met formally with his protégé/mentee, but stopped by often to see if she needed anything. The protégé/mentee told the program administrator that it was because of his mentoring that she was able to get on board quickly, learn the history and meet the players of the division. She said she saved months trying to learn these things on her own. Data like this can be translated into valuable *information*.

Information results when the links to the business case can be made using the data gathered. Since mentoring relationships are based on dialogue, however, it can be difficult to come up with factual data.

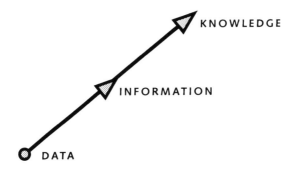

Knowledge. Some of the payoff of a mentoring program comes long after the program ends. That's why it's important to think about metrics from the very beginning. By thinking about it at the outset, your can turn that information into *knowledge* by integrating it into other critical success factors of your organization. When information is transformed into knowledge, it becomes valuable and your mentoring program will be seen as a necessary element for shaping the organization's future, and its true worth will be recognized.

When measuring success, it's also important to make sure that key business leaders learn about the successes of the program. Share as much factual information as you can, supporting it with other "success stories" that may be more difficult to measure. Point out the small achievements as well as the big ones that are more noticeable.

Leaders and stakeholders will want to know:

- Did the investment in resources and time pay off?

- Did it meet the needs it was designed to address?

- What were the "value added" factors derived from the program?

- What are the short-term benefits? Long-term?

- Did it promote a greater feeling of inclusion on the part of the participants?

What was our goal? Why does it matter?	What did we do?	What was the cost and invest- ment?	What are the results? Payoffs? Benefits?	Are we achieving our goal?

- ► Should this program continue? Was it effective?

- ► Did the participants benefit?

- ► If your organization is seeking to be the "employer of choice," talk about how having a mentoring program in place is a good form of P.R. Stress how mentoring provides support to employees and gives them time to work on their own careers and personal effectiveness as well.

- ► If productivity is a critical business issue, highlight the program's focus on communication and relationship building.

- ► If inclusion is a key driver, compare the level of inclusion participants believed they had before the program started and after it was completed.

The goal in the measurement process is to "connect the dots" in order to interpret the results and spell out the benefits of the mentoring program. In other words, you must show the positive impact mentoring has had, and will continue to have, on the things that are important to the organization. It works like this: If your retention of women and people of color has increased by one year, for example, link this fact to the number of women and people of color who participated in the past year's mentoring program. Or, if you have increased the number of women in management positions over the past two years, see if you can link that number to the number of women participating in mentoring programs.

Here are some common outcomes from mentoring programs that can be helpful in setting up your own measurement plan. (Notice how the metrics and outcomes are linked.)

OUTCOME	METRICS
1. Mentors and protégé/mentees make an investment in their future and the future health of the organization. This investment doesn't stop when the program ends.	▸ Retention/Turnover — Career development — Productivity — Employee involvement
2. Mentors develop an ability to reflect on their personal success factors and develop leadership skills.	▸ Leadership — Career development ▸ Advancement — Training
3. Mentors and protégé/mentees discover their personal strengths and examine their potential.	— High potential candidates — Career development — Promotions — Transition time
4. Protégé/mentees are challenged beyond the program as they work on interim activities and report the results.	▸ Results of immediate application — Performance
5. Pairings create a learning organization where individuals have the knowledge to move across divisions, units and departments.	▸ Career opportunities — Knowledge management ▸ Productivity ▸ Utilization of talent
6. Protégé/mentees gain access to a variety of people and resources in the organization.	▸ Inclusion — Retention/Turnover — Transition/Navigation
7. Participants create a sense of community, knowing that there is a support system.	▸ Recruitment ▸ Retention ▸ Diversity
8. Stronger relationships between individuals of different backgrounds and cultures supports diversity initiatives.	▸ Inclusion ▸ Respect ▸ Retention ▸ Recruitment ▸ Opportunities

Often the data you need is readily available in various departments and in reports that already exist. If you need help, don't hesitate to ask others where to look for existing metrics that you can use to build your case.

As you determine your metrics think about:

- Your measurement framework/model.
- Linking the business benefits to the people benefits.
- Clarifying your assumptions going into the program.
- Noting any challenges or difficulties in implementing the program.
- Combining qualitative data with quantitative data (e.g., collect stories, examples and anecdotal information).
- Showing patterns over time.
- Answering "Why?" and "How does it impact the organization?"
- Correlating mentoring programs with existing programs.

The positive results of a mentoring program may not be immediately apparent, and therefore you should remind participants as well as executive staff that long-term benefits often outnumber the short-term gains. In fact, if measurement is important to your organization, a more longitudinal study may be in order. Conducting a comprehensive study will require that you collect some benchmark data before you begin any implementation of a mentoring program. Then compare that data one or two years after the mentoring program has concluded, and compare this data.

Data That Speaks Volumes

Although we have talked about measuring the success of your mentoring program in terms of business issues such as employee retention, employee satisfaction or career development, the data that speaks volumes comes from the participants themselves and what they have to say about their individual mentoring experiences.

We have emphasized that the real success of a mentoring program is what happens between a mentor and protégé/mentee, and therefore it follows that evaluations from them often provide insights and benefits that were not anticipated. That means it is critical to gather data from the participants to evaluate the program, their relationship with their partners, the payoffs and the challenges. In other words, in order to measure the success of a mentoring program, you need to address both the success of the program as a whole and the success of the individual mentoring relationships. Then you can connect this data to the broader picture to determine the ROI. All of these facets help tell the story.

To gather the data from participants, we suggest using traditional evaluation methods along with additional questions that require narrative comments where participants can really elaborate on their experiences. Typically, tools using a numeric ranking from 1 (low) to 5 (high) are administered to answer a series of questions. We advise you to use questions that dig deeper and require serious evaluation of the experience. In addition, we suggest using open-ended narrative questions to generate anecdotal comments. These questions can be in the form of an instrument, either electronic or paper or collected through an interview conducted by the program administrator. Here are some sample questions:

1-Strongly Disagree 2-Disagree 3-Not Sure 4-Agree 5-Strongly Agree

The Program

The goals and objectives of the program were clearly defined.	1 2 3 4 5
I felt supported in this mentoring program from my manager.	1 2 3 4 5
The structure of the program made it easy to perform my role in this relationship.	1 2 3 4 5
The match between my mentoring partner and I worked.	1 2 3 4 5

The Relationship

We have met regularly.	1 2 3 4 5
We had meaningful conversations.	1 2 3 4 5
We came prepared to use the time effectively.	1 2 3 4 5
We were confident about what to do when we started.	1 2 3 4 5
The match between my mentoring partner and I met my needs.	1 2 3 4 5
My mentor understood what I was saying.	1 2 3 4 5
My protégé/mentee understood what I was saying.	1 2 3 4 5

Benefits and Learnings

As a result of this mentoring relationship:

I have grown.	1 2 3 4 5
I feel better about my career.	1 2 3 4 5
I feel more concerned about my career.	1 2 3 4 5
I feel more a part of the organization.	1 2 3 4 5
I feel it was worth my time and effort.	1 2 3 4 5

Narrative Questions

What has been the greatest benefit you received from this experience?

What was the most beneficial thing you learned from your mentoring relationship?

What were the greatest challenges?

What conversations still need to take place?

(See the Appendix for additional samples.)

Below are examples of narrative comments provided by participants who have used ProGroup's dialogue guides, *ConnectionPairs* and *MentorPairs* in a client organization.

Note that these honest and informal comments are exactly the type of "sound bytes" that will help create momentum for your program, demonstrate value to the organization and attract new participants, especially mentors. They will also help you link the program to "the big picture."

> ▸ "I like how the topics are good for all areas of life. This has been an excellent confidence booster. Because my mentor is very different from me, I have gained valuable experience working with someone I would have previously avoided."

> ▸ "I like this program because it gives us a closer look at our attitudes towards our jobs, etc. I have learned a lot about how to deal with different situations, people and moods. I also liked the fact that I've realized what my strengths are and how to let them shine, and what my weaknesses are and how to effectively improve them."

> *(Notice the quote below refers to a transitional mentoring program for newer employees.)*

> ▸ "This gives a new employee an opportunity to get more comfortable with their environment. It helps them be more self sufficient because it gives them the skills to be more effective in becoming part of a team."

> *(Notice the following comment comes from a program administrator of a navigational program.)*

> ▸ "Most protégés felt the mentors were helping in all aspects of life. Protégés also expressed that

they have a better handle on what the options are in the company in terms of career moves (such as mapping out a plan of career growth). Some commented they are learning about the company's unknown (policies, practices, unwritten rules and norms) and how to get from point A to point B. They are also thankful for getting career advice, advice on opportunities and résumé-building advice."

One of our clients has taken an innovative and highly effective approach to evaluation that you may want to use yourself. By using ProGroup's content-specific dialogue guides as the foundation for his program, he was able to create a problem-based evaluation. Specifically, in the beginning, he gave protégé/mentees problems related to a specific topic that would be discussed in the course of the mentoring relationship and asked them to solve these problems as they progressed through the program.

Usually these problems were related to a career challenge and required that protégé/mentees put into practice some of the theories they were discussing with their mentors. Protégé/mentees were asked to solve the problems to the best of their ability, then the program administrator gathered the responses after each session. At the end of the nine-month interaction, he once again gave them the same problems and they solved them using their newly developed skills. The comparison between the first approach to the problem and the second was significant. Since he was able to demonstrate that learning had occurred by utilizing this effective evaluation method, he is considered a hero in his organization.

As you determine your metrics think about:

- Articulating the benefits to the individuals involved, as well as benefits to the organization

- Using a measurement framework/model

- Linking the business benefits to the people benefits
- Clarifying your assumptions going into the program
- Noting any challenges or difficulties in implementing the program
- Combining qualitative data with quantitative data (collect stories, examples, mentor/protégé/mentee evaluations, and anecdotal information)
- Showing patterns over time
- Answering "Why?" and "How does it impact individuals and the organization?"
- Correlating mentoring programs with existing programs

The positive results of a mentoring program may not be immediately apparent, and therefore you should remind participants as well as executive staff that long-term benefits often outnumber the short-term gains. In fact, if measurement is important to your organization, a more longitudinal study may be in order. Conducting a comprehensive study will require that you collect some benchmarking data before you begin any implementation of a mentoring program. Then compare that data one or two years after the mentoring program has concluded.

In Conclusion

We have traveled throughout the country training, lecturing and listening to hundreds of people, and wherever we go we hear the same thing over and over again—getting a mentoring program *started* is the main challenge. So, if you are feeling this way, remember that you are not alone.

This last chapter was deliberately named "Measuring Success" because we believe that by taking the time to read this book, applying some of its principles and considering new ways to improve your program, you will be a success, and your program will be a success as well.

As you move forward, keep these things in mind: get your pairs off to a good start and they will do the work for you; nurture the relationships and equip them with the right tools. If you do these things, the program will be a success, and as a side benefit, you will likely become a hero in your organization. But more importantly, you will be positively impacting the lives of your co-workers as they create relationships that are meaningful and important to their success. That means everyone wins.

Sample Evaluation Questions

Mentoring Program Evaluation

DATE _____

MENTOR NAME _____

PROTÉGÉ/MENTEE NAME _____

Please check one: I am a _____Mentor _____Protégé/Mentee

Instructions

1. Please answer all questions using a scale of 1-5.

   1-Strongly Disagree   4-Agree
   2-Disagree   5-Strongly Agree
   3-Not Sure

2. Circle the number in the columns provided.
3. In the Narrative Questions section, please write in a response.
4. In order to help make the program stronger, please be
   as candid as possible.

The Program

1. The goals and objectives of the program were clearly defined.   1 2 3 4 5
2. I felt supported in this mentoring program from my manager.   1 2 3 4 5
3. The structure of the program made it easy to perform   1 2 3 4 5
   my role in this relationship.
4. The program requirements were just right.   1 2 3 4 5
5. The time commitment for each interaction was just right.   1 2 3 4 5
6. The match between my mentoring partner and I worked.   1 2 3 4 5
7. I believe the program will benefit the organization.   1 2 3 4 5
8. I felt supported by the program administrator.   1 2 3 4 5
9. The overall expected outcomes for the program were realistic.   1 2 3 4 5
10. The program worked for me.   1 2 3 4 5

The Relationship

1. The match between my mentoring partner and I met my needs.   1 2 3 4 5
2. We have met regularly.   1 2 3 4 5
3. We came prepared to use the time effectively.   1 2 3 4 5

continued on next page

4. We were confident about what to do when we started.   1 2 3 4 5
5. My mentor understood what I was saying.   1 2 3 4 5
6. My protégé/mentee understood what I was saying.   1 2 3 4 5
7. I experienced learning and growth during the process.   1 2 3 4 5
8. We were open and honest with each other.   1 2 3 4 5
9. We had meaningful conversations.   1 2 3 4 5
10. My mentor offered guidance and knowledge.   1 2 3 4 5
11. My mentor could be called a "developer of people."   1 2 3 4 5
12. My protégé/mentee shared concerns and asked   1 2 3 4 5
    good questions.
13. My protégé/mentee enlightened me.   1 2 3 4 5
14. This relationship will continue beyond the formal process.   1 2 3 4 5

Benefits and Learnings

1. As a result of this mentoring relationship:
   I have grown.   1 2 3 4 5
   I feel better about my career.   1 2 3 4 5
   I feel more concerned about my career.   1 2 3 4 5
   I feel more a part of the organization.   1 2 3 4 5
   I feel it was worth my time and effort.   1 2 3 4 5
2. The rules for success, both unwritten and written,   1 2 3 4 5
   were explored and considered.
3. Developmental areas were defined and   1 2 3 4 5
   recommendations made.
4. This experience increased my effectiveness.   1 2 3 4 5

Narrative Questions

What has been the greatest benefit you received from this experience?
What were the greatest challenges?
What conversations still need to take place?

Please provide specifics about the mentoring relationship:
Strengths of the relationship_____

_____

Weaknesses_____
Recommendations_____

Please provide specifics about the program:
Strengths_____
Weaknesses_____
Do you have any recommendations that might improve the program?

_____

Sample Mentor Letter

Below is a sample letter you can use and modify when contacting potential mentors within your organization.

Dear (*fill in name*):

As you may be aware, our (*Diversity Committee/Human Resources Department/Training Department, etc.*) is very excited about a new mentoring program we will be implementing (*include date here*). Currently, I am seeking candidates to serve as mentors for the program. With your experience and skill at making people feel right at home, you were someone who immediately came to mind.

The program will be a wonderful opportunity for longer-term employees to support newer hires in their ongoing orientation to the company. For the duration of the program, you will be paired with a protégé/mentee, who is a newer hire with the company. The program, is a (*fill in length of time*) program with excellent dialogue guides and support materials.

I anticipate the time commitment for mentors and their protégé/mentees to be (*fill in time*).

I will stop by later this week to talk with you in person. I hope you will consider applying.

Sincerely,

(*your name*)
(*your job title*)

Sample Protégé/Mentee Letter

Below is a sample letter you can use and modify when contacting potential protégé/mentees within your organization.

Dear (*fill in name*):

As you may be aware, our (*Diversity Committee/Human Resources Department/Training Department, etc.*) is very excited about a new mentoring program we will be implementing (*include date here*). Currently, I am seeking candidates from among the newer hires to participate as protégé/mentees in the program. With your enthusiasm and positive attitude, I think you would be an excellent candidate.

The program will be a wonderful opportunity for newer hires to receive support in their ongoing orientation to the company. For the duration of the program, you will be paired with a mentor, who is a longer-term employee with the company. The program, is a (*fill in length of time*) program with excellent dialogue guides and support materials. I anticipate the time commitment to be (*fill in time*).

I will stop by later this week to talk with you in person. I hope you will consider applying.

Sincerely,

(*your name*)
(*your job title*)

Sample Nominee Request

The sample nominee request form below should be distributed to managers, supervisors and shift leaders as a way to generate names of potential protégé/mentees.

NOMINEE NAME _____

YOUR NAME _____

DEPARTMENT_____

YOUR PHONE _____

YOUR E-MAIL ADDRESS _____

YOUR RELATIONSHIP TO NOMINEE: Manager
    Supervisor
    Shift Leader

Why do you believe this program would benefit the nominee?

Would it be difficult for the nominee to participate in the program if selected?

Do you have any questions for the selection committee?

We anticipate receiving many nominations and wish that we could accommodate everyone. However, we are only able to include (*include number here*) at this time. If your nominee is invited to an interview, it does not necessarily guarantee inclusion in the program. Thank you for your support!

Sample General Announcement

REQUEST FOR NOMINATIONS

The (*name of company*) will be introducing a new mentoring program at the beginning of the next quarter. Candidates for both mentors and protégé/mentees are requested. The program will last (*duration of time*), and includes excellent dialogue guides and support materials. The time commitment for the program is estimated to be (*fill in time*).

We are asking all employees to consider nominating themselves to be protégé/mentee candidates. (Mentor candidates will be chosen by the selection team.) The program is designed to develop personal effectiveness and is an exciting opportunity for newer hires or longer-term employees who feel they would benefit from a structured mentoring relationship.

Please complete the following and return to:
(*your name and contact information*)

NOMINEE NAME _____

DEPARTMENT_____

PHONE _____

YOUR E-MAIL ADDRESS _____

Why do you believe this program would benefit you?

Would it be difficult for you to participate in the program if you are selected?

Do you have any questions about the program?

We anticipate receiving many nominations and wish that we could accommodate everyone. However, we are only able to include (*add number here*) at this time. If you are invited to an interview, it does not necessarily guarantee your inclusion in the program. Thank you for your interest and support!

Pre-Interview Questionnaire

Name: Title:

Department: Manager:

Phone: E-mail:

---

1. Please describe your job history to date or submit a copy of an updated résumé.

2. What types of experiences (work related or other) do you have to offer the mentoring partnership?

3. What do you hope to gain through participating in this program?

4. What would you want the organization to gain from your participation in the program?

5. What do you believe will be the keys to a successful mentoring partnership?

6. Have you ever been involved in a mentoring relationship? If so, what were your impressions?

7. What are you looking for in a mentor? (Consider personality type, as well as knowledge.)

8. What questions, if any, do you have about participating in this mentoring program?

You will be contacted sometime between (*fill in dates*) to schedule an interview prior to the matching session. Please return this completed questionnaire to (*name of program administrator*) via e-mail at (*fill in e-mail address*) or interoffice mail prior to your interview.

Mentor/Mentee Interview Guide

Here are several questions to ask in an interview that will help you in the selection and matching process. (Try to gather all the information during one interview session to make the process more efficient.)

Name: Title:

Department: Manager:

Phone: E-mail:

The Program

What do you hope to gain through participating in this program?

What would you want the organization to gain from this program?

What one outcome of this program would make it worth your time and energy?

About You

Tell me about your background. Where did you grow up? Describe your family.

What are some of your interests and hobbies?

Use a few words to describe yourself.

How would those close to you describe you?

What are your strongest personal values?

continued on next page

The Matching

Have you ever participated in a mentoring program before?
If so, tell me about it.

What do you believe will be the keys to a successful partnership
in this program?

What are you looking for in a mentor? (i.e., function, issues,
experiences) Why?

Describe your ideal mentor (protégé/mentee).

What questions or concerns, if any, do you have about
participating in this program?

What questions or concerns, if any, do you have about working
with someone of a different gender, culture or background?

Are there certain people you find difficult to work with?

Do you have any closing thoughts about the program?
The matching?

INDEX